Challenge & Change

A World Study after 1900

FOUNDATION

JOHN D. CLARE

Hodder & Stoughton

A MEMBER OF THE HODDER HEADLINE GROUP

Acknowledgements

The front cover shows Nelson Mandela reproduced courtesy of Camera Press/H Lindgren, and celebrations on top of the Berlin Wall on 10 November 1989, reproduced courtesy of Associated Press, Berlin.

The publishers would like to thank the following individuals, institutions and companies for permission to reproduce copyright illustrations in this book:
AKG, p2(Le Petit Journal, 13th May 1906 'Les Manifestations du 1 Mai a Paris'), pp 68, 69; AKG/Erich Lessing, p 34bl(*Morning of the Motherland*, by Fyodor Schurpin, 1949); AKG/John Heartfield © DACS, 2000 ('The Meaning of the Hitler Salute – millions are behind me', AIZ Magazine cover, vol. 11, no. 42, 16th Oct l932), p37r; Amalgamated Engineering & Electrical Union (AEEU), Esher, p45b; Anti-Slavery International, p3t/93t(NNRU LN HKJI); Associated Press, pp84t, 85tl; Associated Press/Jean-Marc Bouju, p73; Associated Press/Topham, p90l; Associated Press/Greg Marinovitch, p82b; Bildarchiv Osterreichische Nationalbibliothek, p12t(155.P74/BR), p12b (RV 35PO/B); Bildarchiv Preussischer Kulturbesitz, p38t(F14095)&b(F4898), p40c(F8437); Bilderdienst Suddeutscher Verlag, p36; Bodleian Library, University of Oxford: John Johnson collection: Electricity and Electrical Applicances 3, p46t; Bundesarchiv, Koblenz, p40l(poster for the film *The Eternal Jew*); Camera Press, p88t&b, Camera Press/Jonathan Haddock, p89, Camera Press/Robbie King, p82t; Corbis/Baci, p93b; Corbis/Bettmann, pp49t&b, 84bl, 85br; Corbis/Leif Skoogfors, p92tr; Corbis/Peter Turnley, p74r; Corbis/Nazima Kowall, p81r; Corbis/Underwood & Underwood, p46b; Chicago Historical Society, p48b(neg ICHi-30046 (detail), photographer Jun Fujita); David King Collection, pp 29t&b, 30l&c(stills from Eisenstein's film *October*, 1927), 32, 34t&bl, p35(*Memorable Occasion*, 1936), 53b, p78b(*Krokodil*, Issue no 2, 1952); D.C. Thomson & Co Ltd/ 'Commando' war stories, p54; Dod Miller/Network Photographers, p91b; Harris/© Times Newspapers Ltd, p80l(*The Times*, front page 18.1.99); H-Burkard/ Bilderberg/ Network Photographers, p90r; Hulton Getty, pp4t, 10, 25, 44t&b, 45t, 50/92, 51, 56b, 57b, 70, 71, 85bl; Imperial War Museum p14t(Q33128), p14b, p14l(Q 33161), p15t(POS 327), p15r(Q 70864), p17t&b, p18, p19(MH 30895), p20Q11586), p21(3539, neg POS70), p24t(2722 neg Q80362), p24b(Q55013), p 37tl(HU51084), p39(HU7612), p40r(MH11470), p41(2564), p56t(HU44272), p60t(3188); Library of Congress, Washington, p47(LC-USZC4-6032), p48t/92tl(LC-USZC-4-2426); London Fire Brigade, p57t; Magyar Nemzeti Galeria, Budapest/ Bridgeman Art Library, *Stalin in the Kremlin* by Fedor Pavlovic Resetnikov (1906-83), Magyar Nemzeti Galeria, Budapest/ Bridgeman Art Library © State Tretyakov Gallery, Moscow p60b; Marianna Belova © DACS/RAO, Moscow, 1999, Stalin as War Leader by Petr Lekseevich Belov, © DACS 2000, 1980s, p61; Mary Evans/Fawcett Library pp4b, 5; National Army Museum, London, courtesy of the Director, p 7; Nguyen Kong/Associated Press, p84bl; Novosti (London), p 59t; Peter Newark's Military Pictures, p 11(*The Canadians at Ypres* by W.B. Wollen, 1915), p 53t, p 65(front page of *Collier's Magazine*, Dec 12, 1942, by Arthur Szyk); PA News/David Jones, p81l; PA News/Tony Harris, p92b; Popperfoto, p75tr; Popperfoto/Reuters, p74l(Source: International Defence & Aid Fund for South Africa), pp 75t, 80r, 91tl&tr; Ronald Grant Archive, p6(still from *Ghandi*, 1982), p30br(still from Eisenstein's film October, 1927), Ronald Grant Archive & David James © 1998 TM & Dreamworks, p 62(still from *Saving Private Ryan*, 1998); Solo Syndication Ltd p 6r; The Museum of London, p 3b(CL99/3832, *The Bayswater Omnibus* by G.W. Joy, 1895); TRH/Robert Hunt Library, p58t, 59b; Ullstein Bilderdienst, p42; United Nations, p83.

(key: r right; l left; t top; c centre; b below)

We are unable to trace the following and would be grateful for any information that would enable us to do so, p 33, 66, 75b, 79.

Picture research by Rebecca Teevan.

The publishers would also like to thank the following for permission to reproduce material in this book:
Extracts from *Timewatch* in 1988 reproduced with permission of BBC Licensing; The extract from *Out of the Doll's House* by Angela Holdsworth reprinted on page 50 is reproduced with the permission of BBC Worldwide Limited. Copyright © Angela Holdsworth 1988; *Truman* by Roy Jenkins, HarperCollins, 1986, reproduced by permission of Lord Jenkins; *Ten Days that Shook the World* by John Reed, Lawrence & Wishart, London 1961 (first published in England by the Communist Party of Great Britain, 1926), reproduced by permission of Lawrence & Wishart; *Total War: The Causes and Courses of the Second World War* by Peter Calvocoressi, Guy Wint and John Pritchard (Allen Lane, the Penguin Press, 1972, Revised edition 1989) copyright © Peter Calvocoressi, 1972, 1989, reproduced by permission of Penguin Books Ltd; *Death's Men: Soldiers of the Great War* by Dennis Winter (Allen Lane, 1978) copyright © Dennis Winter, 1978, reproduced by permission of Penguin Books Ltd; *The First Day of the Somme: 1 July 1916* by Martin Middlebrook (Penguin Books, 1984) copyright © Martin Middlebrook, 1984, reproduced by permission of Penguin Books Ltd; *A Century of Women: A History of Women in Britain and the United States* by Sheila Rowbotham (Penguin Books, 1997) copyright © Sheila Rowbotham, 1997, reproduced by permission of Penguin Books Ltd; Sutton Publishing Limited for the extract from *Women in the 1920's* by Pamela Horn, Sutton Publishing Ltd, 1995; *The Informed Heart* by B Bettelhelm, Thames and Hudson Ltd, 1960, reproduced by permission of Thames & Hudson Ltd; From *The Great War* by Jay Winter and Blaine Baggett, copyright © 1996 by Community Television of Southern California. Used by permission of Penguin, a division of Penguin Putnam Inc.; *Purnell's History of the 20th Century*, Macdonald Young Books Ltd reproduced with permission of Wayland Publishers.

Please note that all sources have been adapted to make them more accessible to students.

Every effort has been made to trace and acknowledge ownership of copyright. The publishers will be glad to make suitable arrangements with any copyright holders whom it has not been possible to contact.

Orders: please contact Bookpoint Ltd, 78 Milton Park, Abingdon, Oxon OX14 4TD. Telephone: (44) 01235 827720, Fax: (44) 01235 400454. Lines are open from 9.00 - 6.00, Monday to Saturday, with a 24 hour message answering service. Email address: orders@bookpoint.co.uk

British Library Cataloguing in Publication Data
A catalogue record for this title is available from The British Library

ISBN 0 340 74234 8

First published 2000
Impression number 10 9 8 7 6 5 4 3 2 1
Year 2005 2004 2003 2002 2001 2000

Typeset by Liz Rowe.
Printed in Italy for Hodder & Stoughton Educational, a division of Hodder Headline Plc, 338 Euston Road, London NW1 3BH by Printer Trento, Italy.

Contents

1 THE WORLD IN 1900

IN THIS CHAPTER YOU WILL LEARN:

- **THREE groups of people who challenged the old order in 1900;**
- **TEN ways suffragettes tried to get the vote.**

NEW WORDS

Communists: want wealth shared more equally.

anti-colonialists: people in a colony who want to be free.

Suffragists: women in Britain who wanted the vote by peaceful means.

foreigners: people from a different country

police

Asia

Belgium

navies

A changing Europe

In 1900 most of Europe was still ruled by powerful kings. They used their armies and secret police to stay in power.

But, all over Europe, the industrial revolution was changing things. Big towns were growing up. Many workers lived in these towns. Most of them were very poor. Many became ***Communists***, and wanted to overthrow their government by a revolution.

A changing world

In 1900 the countries of Europe still ruled most of Africa and Asia. They used their navies and weapons to keep power. They used their colonies to give them cheap food and raw materials. The colonies made the countries of Europe rich.

But in the colonies, groups of native people – called ***anti-colonialists*** – hated the foreigners and wanted to be free.

SOURCE A

▲ *This French picture shows workers being stopped by the army.*

Changing Britain

Unlike most of the countries of Europe, Britain was ruled by a Parliament elected by all men over the age of 21. But most men did not believe that a woman was as good as a man, and women still did not have the vote.

A group of women – called the *Suffragists* – said that women were equal to men, and that they should have the vote.

In 1900, millions of Indians died in a great famine. The British government, which ruled India, refused to cut spending on the army to feed the starving Indians.

In 1900, only 5 countries in the world had Parliaments. Britain owned 1/5th of all the land in the world. In Britain, 3% of the people had 33% of the money.

SOURCE B

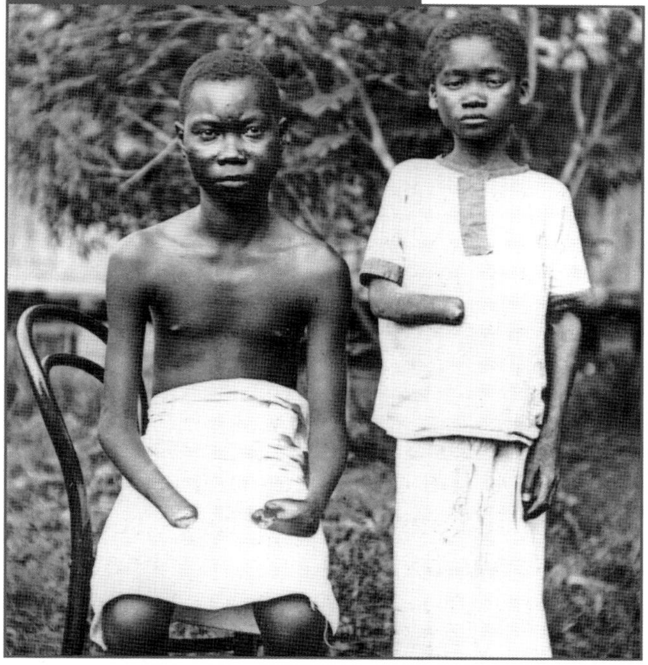

The Congo, in Africa, was ruled by Belgium. These African workers have been punished by having their hands cut off.

SOURCE C

This painting shows people on a London bus in the 1900s.

Tasks

1. Look at **Source C**. List all the differences between the man and the women, and between the rich and the poor.

2. Imagine you are either a Communist, an anti-colonialist or a suffragist. Choose either **Source A**, **B** or **C** and make up a short speech to give to the rest of the class, saying how you think it shows a great injustice.

?
Votes for Women!

Was Mrs Pankhurst right?

Suffragists, Suffragettes

The Suffragists wanted the vote, but they tried to get it peacefully. In 1903, they tried to get Parliament to pass a law giving them the vote. The MPs did not even vote on the bill.

So, in 1903, Mrs Emmeline Pankhurst started the Suffragettes. She said that women should break the law to get the vote.

The Suffragettes:

1. Shouted out at meetings,
2. Went on marches,
3. Chained themselves to railings,
4. Refused to pay fines,
5. Attacked the police,
6. Broke shop windows,
7. Slashed paintings,
8. Burned down churches,
9. Threw bombs,
10. Went on hunger strike when they were put in prison.

SOURCE A

Mrs Pankhurst is arrested.

In the 1913 Derby horse race one Suffragette, Emily Davison, was killed when she threw herself under the king's horse. Many men were angry, because the king's horse was a good horse.

SOURCE B

What a Woman may be, and yet not have the Vote
MAYOR
NURSE
MOTHER
DOCTOR or TEACHER
FACTORY HAND
What a Man may have been, & yet not lose the Vote
CONVICT
LUNATIC
Proprietor of white Slaves
Unfit for Service
DRUNKARD

This poster from 1912 says women should have the vote.

NEW WORDS

Suffragettes: broke the law to get the vote.

argument

politics

SOURCE C

Ladies. If we had the power, we would give you the vote now. Please do not smash these windows.

A poster in a London shop in 1912.

SOURCE E

Burning down our churches was not a very good way to persuade us.

Written by the Bishop of London in 1918.

SOURCE F

The broken window is the best argument in politics.

Said by Mrs Pankhurst.

New Zealand gave women the vote in 1893. Women in Switzerland were not given the vote until 1971.

SOURCE D

To many men, the Suffragettes were a joke. What does this picture say that really made the Suffragettes angry?

The War and the Vote

During the First World War, the Suffragettes stopped their protests.

Women joined the army as cooks and drivers. They became nurses. At home, they made shells, carried coal and mended roads.

By 1918, nobody could say that women were not as good as men. In 1918, women over the age of 30 (and in 1928, all women over 21) were given the vote.

Tasks

1. Look at **Sources A** and **B**.

- Which will get the best publicity?
- Which will be more likely to convince people that women should have the vote?

2. Look at **Sources C**, **D** and **E**. How did men react to the Suffragettes' tactics?

3. Was Mrs Pankhurst right in **Source F** – did the Suffragettes get women the vote?

4. Hold an imaginary meeting between some Suffragettes and some Suffragists. The Suffragettes describe what they want to do, and why. The Suffragists try to persuade them that their tactics would be a mistake.

Amritsar

Your Mission: to advise the Queen when she visits India. Should she apologise for the Amritsar Massacre?

Amritsar

On 14 October 1997, Queen Elizabeth II went to Amritsar in northern India.

The Queen's visit caused a lot of trouble. Many Indians said she should not have gone. Others said that she should have made a speech.

Because, on 13 April 1919, British soldiers in Amritsar had shot dead 379 unarmed Indians.

General Reginald Dyer 1864–1927

SOURCE A

The Amritsar Massacre – a picture from a modern film.

SOURCE B

I knew there was going to be trouble. Amritsar was the centre of a rebellion. The people who met (on 13 April) were declaring war because they thought I would not dare to stop them. It was a horrible job for me to do. But I made up my mind to fire.

General Dyer, giving his side of the story.

FACTFILE

1919
Many Indians wanted independence, but their leaders said that they would not try to get it by a revolution.

6 April 1919
There were riots all over northern India.

10 April 1919
The British government arrested two Indian leaders. A crowd of 20,000 Indians went to ask where they were. British troops opened fire, killing about 20. The Indians rioted, killing 4 British people.

11 April 1919
General Dyer went to Amritsar.

13 April 1919: morning
British troops went round parts of the town telling people that they could not hold protest meetings.

13 April 1919: afternoon
A big crowd met in a local park. Some people had gone to hold a protest meeting, but most had just gone because it was a holy day.

Dyer took a troop of soldiers. Without warning, they fired into the crowd for 10 minutes, killing 379.

SOURCE C

We were not rebelling against the British government. The riots were caused by what the British did.

Indians' leaders give their side of the story.

SOURCE D

I believe it was needed to stop the trouble – not only in Amritsar, but in the whole area round about – which was my duty.

Sir Michael O'Dwyer, British governor of northern India.

SOURCE E

After 13 April, British soldiers attacked Indians all over India. Here, they force a man to crawl down a street in Amritsar. Indians had to bow to every British person they met.

SOURCE F

The British government is the Devil! When a government kills its own unarmed people, then it no longer has a right to rule.

Said by Gandhi, the Indian leader.

NEW WORDS

crowd
official

SOURCE G

The Queen is not going to say she is sorry, but she is going to lay some flowers.

The British government said this before the Queen went to India in October 1997.

Tasks

1. Read **Source B**. Why did Dyer say he fired on the crowd? Are there any facts in the Factfile which suggest that he was justified?

2. Read **Source C**. What did the Indian leaders say? Are there any facts in the Factfile which suggest that they were right?

3. Read **Source D**. Why did the British treat the Indians as harshly as they did in **Source E**?

4. Read **Source F**. Why did Gandhi say such very different things about the Amritsar massacre from O'Dwyer (in **Source D**)?

5. Read **Source G**. Do you think the British government was wrong – should the Queen say that Britain is sorry?

6. You are the Queen's speech writer. Write a short speech for her to give at Amritsar.

2 THE ORIGINS OF WORLD WAR ONE

IN THIS CHAPTER YOU WILL LEARN:

- TWELVE steps to World War One;
- FIVE reasons the Schlieffen Plan failed.

Ready for war

In 1914, Europe was split into two sides – the Triple Alliance (of Germany, Austria-Hungary and Italy) and the Triple Entente (an alliance of France, Russia and Britain). The two sides hated each other.

All that was needed was a small spark to set the world at war.

The picture shows how one small thing caused a world war.

NEW WORDS

alliance, entente: where two countries agree to be **allies** (friends).
student, declare war, afraid

Tasks

1. Using the illustration, make a list of the seven ***key dates*** in 'The Slide to War June–August 1914'.

2. List SEVEN countries involved in the start of the First World War. Look at the 'thought bubbles' for each country and decide – did it HAVE to go to war, or did it WANT to go to war?

1.
28 June 1914
Archduke Franz Ferdinand of Austria was shot by a student.
2.
Serbia did this! We must punish Serbia.
3.
23 July 1914
Austria demanded that Austrian police go into Serbia – or Austria would declare war.
4.
This is just a trick to take over Serbia.
5.
24 July 1914
Serbia asked Russia for help.
6.
This is not a fair war. Austria is trying to take over Serbia.
7.
31 July 1914
Russia called up its army.
8.
Russia and France are allies. We will have to fight them both at the same time. Our plan is to fight France first, then Russia. If we move NOW, we can win.
9.
Germany declared war on Russia (1 August 1914) and France (3 August 1914). The German army attacked France, going through Belgium.
13.
Italy will wait. We will join in when we see who is winning.
Germany
Austria
Serbia
Russia
Italy

Why did the Schlieffen Plan fail?

The German army had been expecting a war with France and Russia since 1897. It had a plan to fight them – called the Schlieffen Plan after the general who drew it up. Everything was planned, down to the last soldier!

The Germans thought that Russia would be the real danger. And they thought they could defeat France in six weeks, before the Russian army could get ready. The German army planned to march through Belgium and into France to capture Paris. Then the German troops would be rushed in trains to go to fight the Russian army.

Alfred von Schlieffen. 1833–1913.

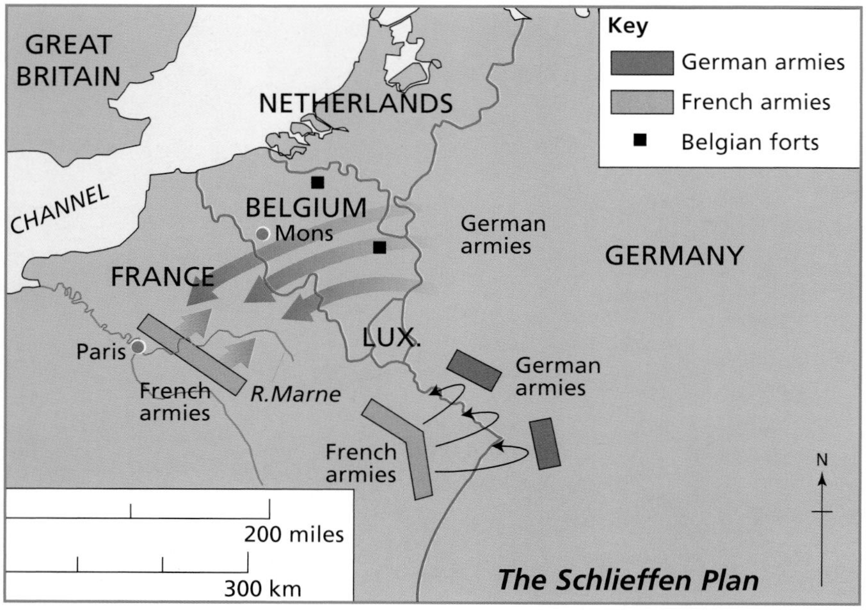

German army movements August to September 1914.

The Schlieffen Plan fails

1. Russia called up her army much faster than the Germans expected
2. Belgium tried to stop the German army, and held it up for three days.
3. Britain declared war. The Germans did not think the British army was any good, but the British held them up at the Battle of Mons.
4. The French army was better than the Germans expected. The French used trains and taxis to get soldiers to the front to fight.

SOURCE A

The Schlieffen Plan failed because Schlieffen forgot that the enemy would fight back.

Written by A.J.P. Taylor, a modern historian.

SOURCE B

The Schlieffen Plan failed because the German soldiers had to march too far. By the battle of the Marne they were too tired. They would have found it hard to get to Paris, even if the French army had not fought them.

Written by Jay Winter, a modern historian.

Schlieffen's biggest mistake

5. The Schlieffen Plan was a plan of attack. The Germans thought that they would win the war by attacking the enemy. But warfare had changed. The attacking soldiers were killed by machine guns and artillery shells.

The Germans joked about the small British army. Asked what he would do if the British army invaded, one German said: 'I would send a policeman to arrest it!'

In September 1914, the German attack failed. The British and the French armies defeated the German army at the battle of the Marne.

The Germans dug trenches. When the British and French tried to attack, they killed them (using machine-guns and artillery shells).

The British and the French armies dug trenches, too.

For the rest of the war, the two sides faced each other like this, with only a few hundred metres of 'No Man's Land' between them.

NEW WORDS

Schlieffen Plan

general, artillery

SOURCE C

This picture shows a German attack in 1915. The Germans had many more soldiers, but they were defeated by the defenders' machine-guns and artillery.

Tasks

1. Do **Sources A** and **B** disagree about why the Plan failed? Looking at *lines 15–33*, which historian do you think got it right?

2. Work in a group. Using the map as a visual aid, prepare a presentation for the rest of the class, explaining why the Plan failed. Mention enemy armies, German mistakes, long marches, new weapons.

Franz Ferdinand's last day

Your Mission: *to produce a report for the Austrian government on the murder of Archduke Franz Ferdinand.*

28 June 1914

Archduke Franz Ferdinand of Austria-Hungary, visited Sarajevo, in Bosnia. Six students waited to kill him. One of them threw a bomb, but failed to kill the Archduke.

The Archduke stopped the visit. But on the way home, his driver pulled up right in front of one of the students, Gavrilo Princip. Franz Ferdinand was shot dead.

Who was to blame?

SOURCE A

The Archduke's car passes along a street in Sarajevo.

SOURCE B

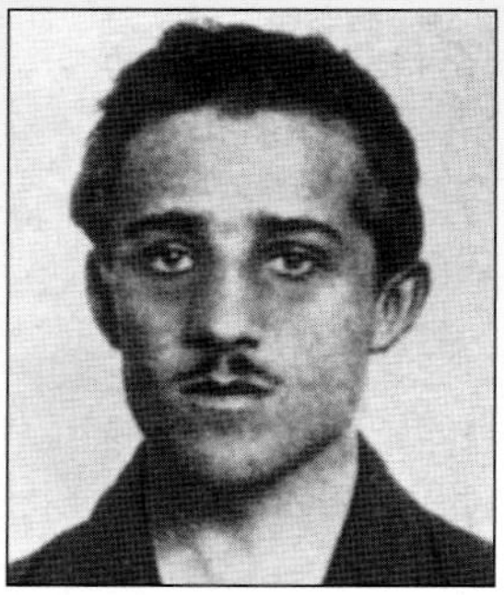

Name: Gavrilo Princip
19 years old
Born: Bosnia
Job: student
Information: May be a member of a group of Bosnian trouble-makers. He has visited Serbia a number of times.

What we know of the murderer.

SOURCE C

I pulled out the gun and fired. I did not take aim. I looked away as I shot. I fired, but I cannot say how many times I shot them – I was too excited.

Princip's story of the murder.

SOURCE D

1910: ***Emperor Franz Joseph visits Sarajevo***

- All roads lined with two rows of soldiers.
- Hundreds of people told to stay at home.

1914: ***Franz Ferdinand visits Sarajevo***

- 70,000 soldiers kept outside the town.
- 120 policemen watch the roads.

Police security for two visits to Sarajevo.

SOURCE E

Security? I do not care at all about it. God will take care of me. Look – someone could jump out and kill me right now! Worrying about it could ruin your life.

What Archduke Franz Ferdinand thought about security.

SOURCE F

This was not done by just one man.

This is Serbia's doing – they want war with Austria-Hungary. We must do something about it. If we do nothing we will have trouble from other races in the Empire. We must go to war against Serbia.

What the Austrian army thought about the murder.

SOURCE G

Security on 28 June will be in God's hands.

What a policeman in Sarajevo thought about security.

SOURCE H

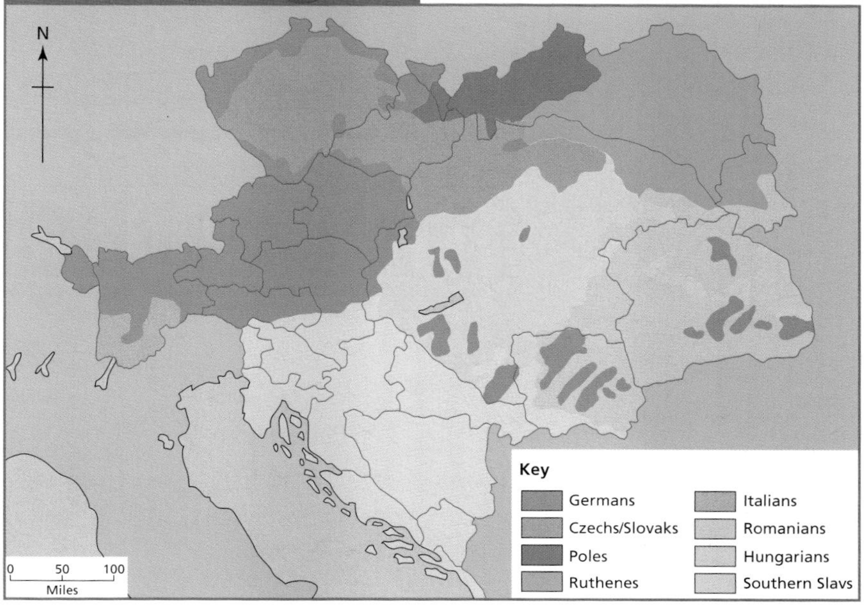

A map of Austria-Hungary, showing the different races. Many of these races wanted to be independent countries.

SOURCE I

Many things prove that Serbia did not order the murder of Franz Ferdinand. The Serbian government did not want him killed.

Serbia had just finished fighting two wars. Only a madman would have wanted to go to war with Austria-Hungary, which was much stronger.

What the Germans thought about the murder.

Tasks

Write a report for the Austrian government about the murder. Answer:

1. Who murdered the Archduke (**Source B**)?

2. Was he a professional hit-man (**Source C**)?

3. Were security arrangements good enough (**Source D**)?

4. Who was to blame for the poor security (**Sources E** and **G**)?

5. Was Serbia behind the murder (**Source I**)?

6. Should Austria-Hungary go to war with Serbia (**Sources F** and **H**)?

Remember to give the evidence which supports your conclusions.

Why did men volunteer?

***Your Mission:* to make a speech, persuading young men from your town to join the army and go to fight in the First World War.**

You live in a small town. The speaker who was going to drum up support for the army has not turned up – ***you*** will have to give the speech, but what will you say?

You look round the room and see five recruitment posters. Each one gives you an idea about why men should join up and fight . . .

Daddy, what did YOU do in the Great War?

NEW WORDS

recruitment, poster, idea

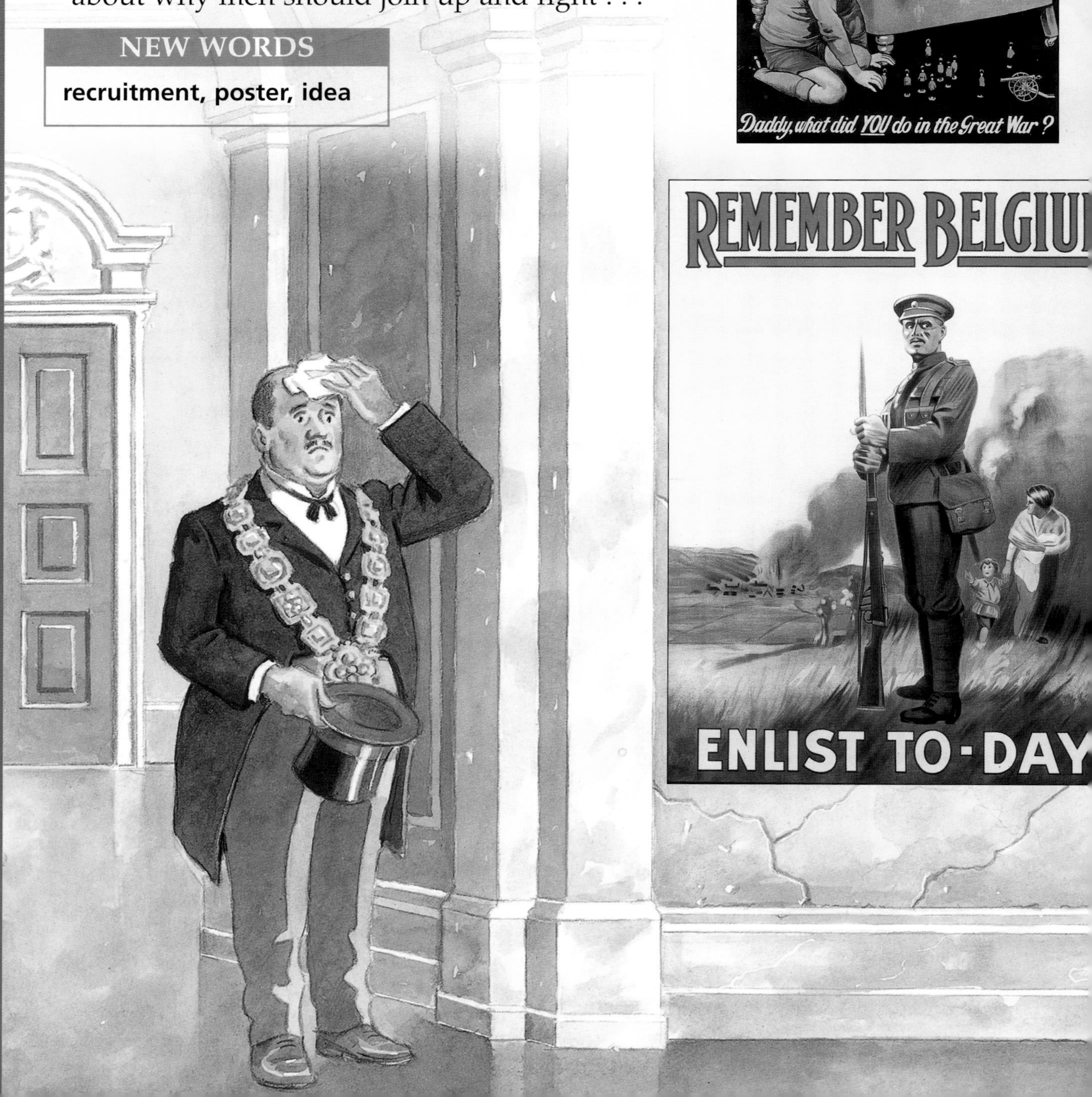

YOUR COUNTRY'S CALL
Isn't this worth fighting for?
ENLIST NOW

Tasks

Work with a partner to work out what you will say:

1. First, think about the five posters. What is the message of each poster? How does it try to persuade men to join up?

2. Now, write a short speech with five points, persuading the young men in the room to join up. Finish with an emotional appeal to them to go to fight in the war.

3. Give your speech to the rest of the class, as though you were really there in 1914.

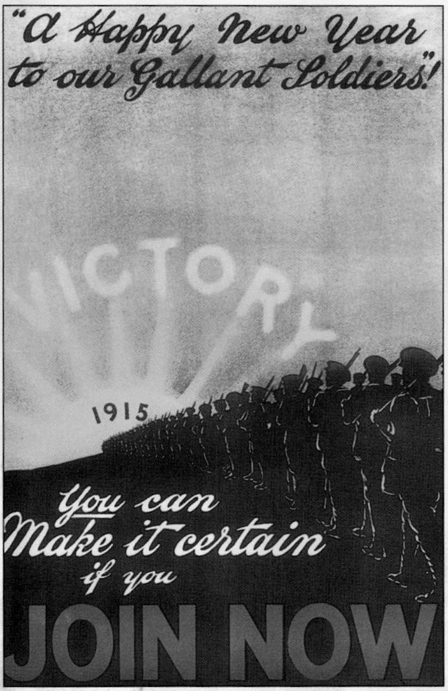
"A Happy New Year to our Gallant Soldiers!"
VICTORY
1915
You can Make it certain if you
JOIN NOW

GO!
IT'S YOUR DUTY LAD
JOIN TO-DAY

3 LIVING AND DYING IN THE TRENCHES

IN THIS CHAPTER YOU WILL LEARN:

- NINE parts of a trench system;
- EIGHT ways you could die in the trenches.

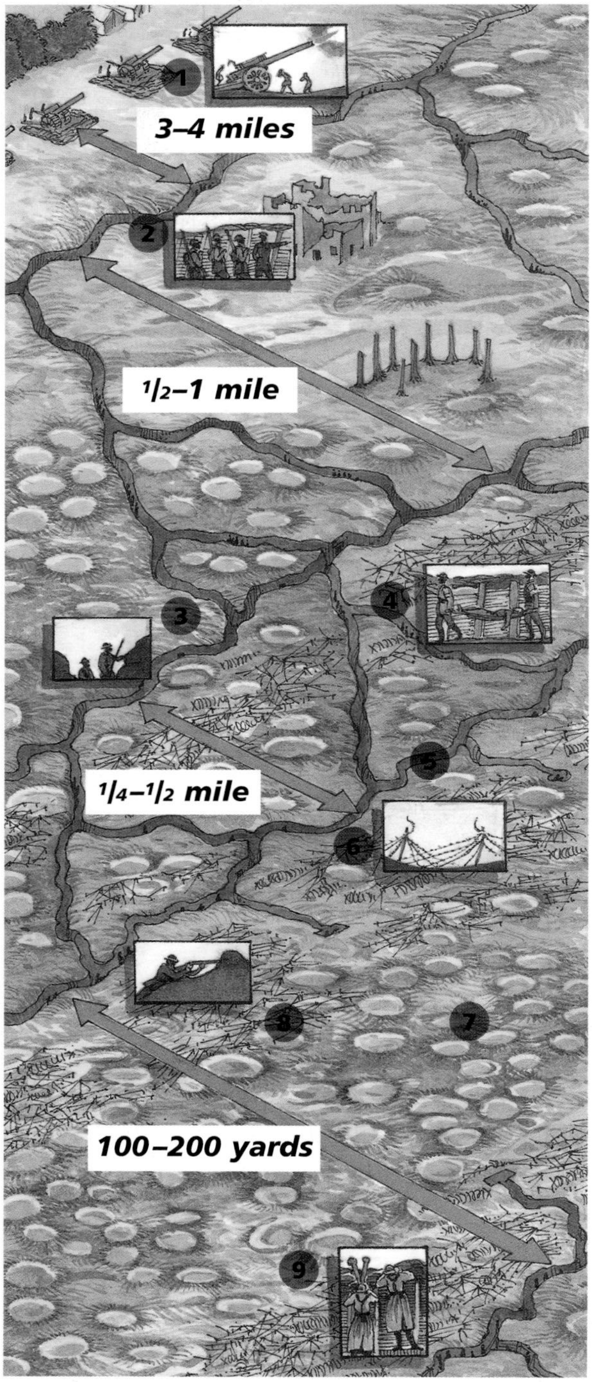

A view of the trenches.

1. Behind the lines: the generals, food and weapons. Also the artillery which fired shells at the German lines.

2. Reserve trenches: used to build up forces for an attack. A soldier might spend 8 days a month here.

3. Support trench: men were put here in case the Germans broke through the front line. Not as dangerous as the front line. A soldier might spend 4 days a month here.

4. Saps: trenches for moving men and food up to the front line.

5. Front-line trench: great danger from attack and sniper fire. A soldier might spend 4 days a month here.

6. Barbed wire: to hold up the enemy. Tin cans hung on the wire to give warning of an attack.

7. No Man's Land: nobody dared to go here during the day, but at night men went out on raids.

8. Listening post: at night a small group of men would go into a crater close to enemy lines to watch what the enemy was doing.

9. German front-line trench: made out of concrete, the Germans went into deep pits to protect them from British shelling.

NEW WORDS

crater: the hole made by an artillery shell.
sniper: hidden gunman.
dug-out: small room where the officers lived.
reserve, month, concrete, dawn, ledge, wound, bayonet

Life in the trenches

The soldiers woke up an hour before dawn. They had to stand by, ready in case of an enemy attack at dawn. Then the rest of the day was spent watching for an enemy attack, or working (digging trenches or filling sandbags).

The worst thing about the trenches were the conditions. Rain turned the soil to mud so deep that a soldier could drown in it. The men were wet all the time. In winter the cold was terrible. Many men became ill – as many men died of ***cold*** and ***disease*** as died in battle. Officers had small dug-outs, but most British soldiers had to try to sleep on a ledge dug out of the side of the trench.

Lice were a great problem, and so were the rats – grown fat from eating the bodies of the dead. Sometimes they attacked sleeping men.

SOURCE A

British soldiers in a flooded sap.

SOURCE B

The cold got into our clothes, our fingers and our bones. It froze our blood. It was weeks before I could feel my toes.

Written by a British soldier in 1917.

SOURCE C

The body of a German soldier rotting in the trenches. Why has his face been eaten away?

SOURCE D

Taking a wounded soldier from the front line.

SOURCE E

9 December 1915:
Foggy. Cool. Hit one man by a tree. Another one 50 yards right – he fell over a log. Then shot 3 men who went to help him.
16 December 1916:
Fine. 16 good shots. 7 known hits and feel sure of 4 more.

Diary of a British sniper.

Death in the trenches

At any time a soldier might be ***hit by a sniper*** – a sniper could kill a man from half a mile away.

Or a soldier could be blown up or buried alive by ***an enemy shell***. The worst thing was shrapnel – the red-hot bits of metal which flew out from an exploding shell. Even if the shell did not kill a man, dirt got into the wounds and he could die later of ***blood-poisoning***.

More men died from shelling than died in battle. Many were sent mad by the fear and the noise.

SOURCE F

There was no hope. His head was smashed. Bits of brain lay in a pool under him...
It took two hours before he died, with lots of men around him and the smell of the blood . . . crying out and gurgling, and a death rattle fit for a book.

The death of a soldier hit by a sniper's bullet.

The biggest gun in World War One was a German gun called Big Bertha. It could fire a shell as big as a car more than 70 miles.

Night in the trenches

Night was the worst time for the men. Both sides sent out raiding parties who would attack enemy lines or try to take prisoners.

Sometimes two raiding parties would meet in No Man's Land, and there would be a quiet, bloody fight to the death using ***knives***, and ***clubs and spades***.

An attack

Generals had only one battle-plan. First they shelled the enemy line. Then they ordered the men to go 'over the top' – to get out of their trench, run across No Man's Land and try to capture the enemy's front-line trench.

The enemy was waiting, with shells and *machine guns*. Millions of men died in these attacks. Even if the attack captured the enemy trench, often the enemy would take it back a few days later – with just as many men killed.

SOURCE G

Old soldiers said that ***bayoneting*** a man was like sticking a knife into butter. But the blade got stuck between the ribs – so they gave the bayonet a half-twist to get it out again.

Written by a modern historian.

SOURCE H

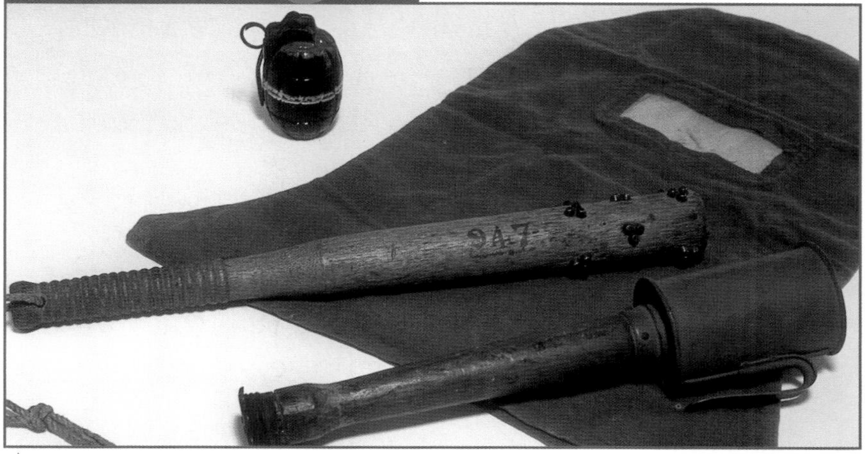

Weapons used in trench raids.

SOURCE I

We're here because
we're here, because
we're here, because
we're here. (x2)

A song sung by British soldiers (to the tune of* Auld Lang Syne*). How did these soldiers feel about the war?

How men felt about the war

At the start of the war, the men had been keen. As the war went on, they came to hate the Germans, and they came to hate the generals who told them to go to their deaths.

During the war, the army told doctors that they were not allowed to say a man had shell-shock. So hundreds of men who had in fact gone mad, were ***shot by a firing squad*** for disobeying orders.

Tasks

1. Look through pages 16–19 and find ***EIGHT ways*** you could die in the trenches.

2. Working in a small group, make up a drama in which an old soldier is questioned by some young men new to the front line. They will ask him about the trench system, the jobs they will do, what conditions they will find in the trenches, enemy artillery and shell-shock, attacking the enemy – and how they will die.

Finally, they will ask him what he feels about the Germans, and about the generals.

New weapons

Gas

22 April 1915: French soldiers near the town of Ypres saw a yellow cloud blowing towards them. They began to choke and die. It was poison gas! The men just threw down their guns and ran away in terror – if the Germans had been ready, they could have broken through and won the war!

As the war went on, the Germans invented new poison gases. The gases burned out the soldiers' lungs, burned their skin to the bone and blinded them.

Before they were given gas-masks, British soldiers protected themselves by urinating on hankies and breathing through them. Scottish soldiers in kilts protected their legs by wearing ladies' drawers.

SOURCE A

Horns would be honked, shell-cases hit, guns shot. And for miles around, in panic, frightened soldiers would wake up and put on their gas masks.

There were as many cases of 'gas-shock' as there were of shell-shock.

▲ ***Written by a modern historian.***

SOURCE B

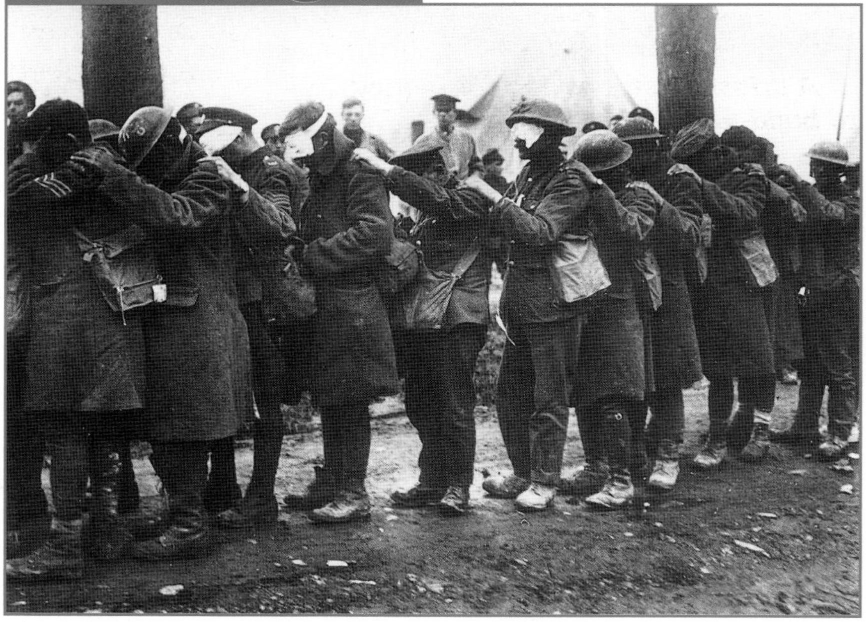

▲ ***British soldiers blinded by a gas attack.***

Problems with gas

Gas had its problems. A change of wind could blow it back onto the attackers. The British quickly gave 300,000 gas masks to their soldiers. They also began to use poison gas themselves.

Gas was not a war-winning weapon. It only made the war more terrible for the ordinary soldier.

SOURCE C

THE TANK
is a travelling fortress
that clears the way for
our soldiers.
It cuts through the wire - under fire
It saves lives
It is *our* War discovery
It is a matter of pride to help to
build Tanks.

A British poster asking for money to build tanks.

SOURCE D

Tanks did not win the war, but they made people at home feel better.

Said on the BBC TV programme Timewatch.

Tanks

15 September 1916: A British officer in an attack during the Battle of the Somme sent in 12 tanks – a new secret weapon. They ran over the German trenches and machine-guns. British soldiers, hiding behind the metal machines, went forward and captured the German trenches. The German soldiers ran away in terror.

One of the tanks stuck at top speed and just kept on going until it ran out of petrol, miles behind German lines – nobody (not even the driver) could stop it.

Problems with tanks

Tanks had many problems. They broke down all the time. They had a top speed of 4 miles an hour. They got stuck in the mud and fell into shell craters. Drivers suffocated or went mad in the heat and fumes inside the tanks.

The Germans soon invented tank-traps, and bullets that could go through the tanks' steel sides. They also invented their own tanks.

Not until the Second World War were tanks a war-winning weapon.

Tasks

1. Write a radio news broadcast such as might have been made in Britain on 23 April 1915. What would it say?

Now write one such as might have been made in Germany on the same day. How would it be different?

2. Do the same for 16 September 1916.

3. Using the information on page 20 (especially **Source B**), and working with a small group of pupils, enact a drama about a group of British soldiers in a gas attack at night.

Breakthrough on the Somme?

Your Mission: to learn from your mistakes!

The first day of the Battle of the Somme has been a disaster. Almost 57,000 men have been lost, dead or wounded. It is your job to examine the reports of what happened (page 23), compared to what was *supposed* to happen (page 22), and to find out WHAT WENT WRONG.

NEW WORDS

Commander-in-Chief

Private

Sergeant

Plan for the Battle of the Somme

TOP SECRET

1. We will gather a huge new army of soldiers.

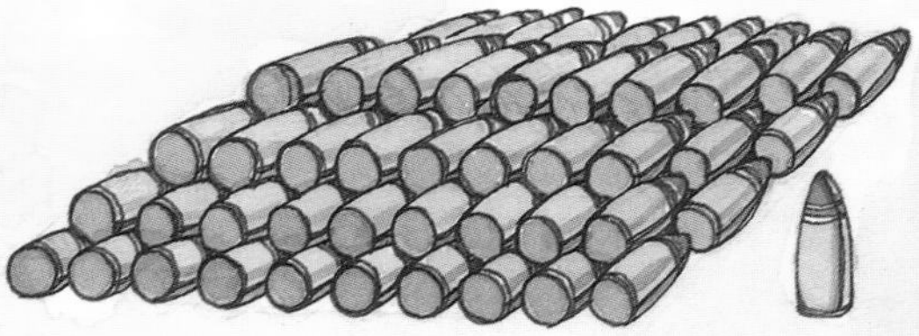

2. Men and supplies will be collected in the reserve trenches.

3. German trenches will be bombarded for 7 days. $1\frac{1}{2}$ million shells will be used.

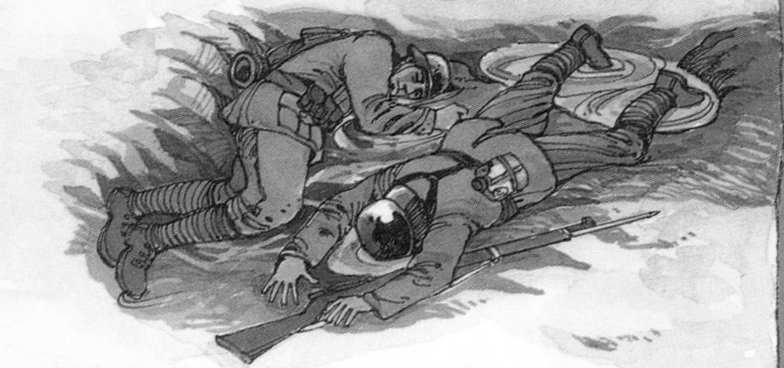

4. The shells will destroy the German dug-outs, shred their barbed wire, and kill most of their soldiers.

5. Ten mines will be dug under German strong points. They will be exploded 2 minutes before the attack.

6. The army will cross No Man's Land walking (so that they can stay in line). They will capture the German trenches.

Signed *Douglas Haig*
COMMANDER-IN-CHIEF
British Army

SOURCE A

The mines were blown at 7.28 am, all except the one at Hawthorn Ridge. This was blown at 7.20 am

This was a mistake. The German artillery started to shell all the British trenches. Their soldiers, too, got ready – they knew an attack was coming.

Written by a modern historian.

SOURCE B

I was in the first wave. Most of all, I remember seeing all the shells which had not exploded.

They were supposed to destroy the German barbed wire, but it was still all there.

Private G.S. Young, who was in the battle.

SOURCE C

We went down into a German dug-out – and found the electric lights still burning. So much for the idea that the artillery would kill the enemy.

Private A. McMullen, who was in the battle.

SOURCE D

When the English came at us, it seemed that we could not stop them. But then we saw that they were walking. We had never seen that before. I saw one officer, walking out in front with his stick .

When we started firing, we did not have to aim – we just fired into them. If they had run, they would have defeated us.

Private Karl Blenk, a German soldier.

SOURCE E

To my left and right I could see long lines of men. Then I heard the rat-tat of machine-guns. By the time I had gone 10 metres there seemed only to be a few men left by me. By the time I had gone 20 metres I was on my own. Then I was hit.

Sergeant Galloway, who was in the battle.

Tasks

1. Choose pupils to play the different soldiers **A–E**. Ask your teacher to be the investigator and to find out from the 'soldiers' what they remember about the battle.

2. Prepare a report about what went wrong. Mention:

a. Which of the six parts of the plan (page 22) did not work? Explain what went wrong.

b. Who was to blame?

c. What advice would you make to stop this happening again?

4 THE END OF THE WAR

IN THIS CHAPTER YOU WILL LEARN:

- **FOUR reasons why Germany lost;**
- **EIGHT terms of the Treaty of Versailles.**

NEW WORDS

Blitzkrieg: a German word meaning 'lightning war'.
Armistice: the ceasefire.
heroes: people who have behaved bravely.

Germany tries to win

In 1917, two things happened.

Firstly, in April, the USA came into the war on Britain's side. They began to get their army ready to send to Europe. Germany knew that, when the Americans came, they would lose the war.

Then, in November, the Russian government fell, and the Russians pulled out of the war. Germany could send the soldiers who had been fighting Russia to the western front in France. They decided to try and win the war in one last attack, before the Americans came.

SOURCE A

An American poster asking men to join the army.

SOURCE B

German stormtroopers go over the top on 21 March 1918.

A last attack?

The German army invented a new way of fighting. Instead of attacking the British trenches along a wide front, they attacked at a few small points. Once they had broken through, they kept going. They called this ***Blitzkrieg***, and the soldiers who did it 'stormtroopers'.

SOURCE C

▲ ***German soldiers go home in 1918 – and are treated like heroes. Many did not think they had lost the war. They thought that the German government had betrayed them.***

The Germans broke through on 21 March 1918. At first they won. But their forces were tired, and they had lost too many men. On 8 August 1918, using fresh American soldiers, tanks and aircraft, the British and French attacked and pushed the German army back.

Inside Germany, too, things were going badly. Since 1914, the British navy had stopped any food getting to Germany by sea. By 1918, German people were living on berries. And when the German government told its navy to go and fight the British, it refused. All over Germany there were strikes and riots.

The Germans could not go on. They asked for a ceasefire (the 'Armistice'). At 11 am on 11 November 1918, the First World War ended.

SOURCE D

The 1918 attack failed, but the Germans lost nothing important. The British and French had not broken through the German line. The German trenches were stronger than ever.

But the Germans knew they had lost. They knew they could not win.

They gave up. They only wanted to end the war.

▲ ***The modern historian, A.J.P Taylor.***

Tasks

1. Germany lost the war for FOUR reasons:

- The US entered the war *(lines 3–7)*,
- The March attack failed *(lines 28–36)*,
- The British blockade *(lines 38–42)*,
- The mutiny of the German navy *(lines 42–46)*.

For each factor, explain HOW it made Germany lose the war.

2. Which do you think was the most important factor?

How did the war affect Germany?

Your Mission: to produce a report for the German government on the Treaty of Versailles.

28 June 1919

The German government is being forced to sign the Treaty of Versailles. You have been asked to get hold of a copy of the Treaty, and to write about how it will affect Germany.

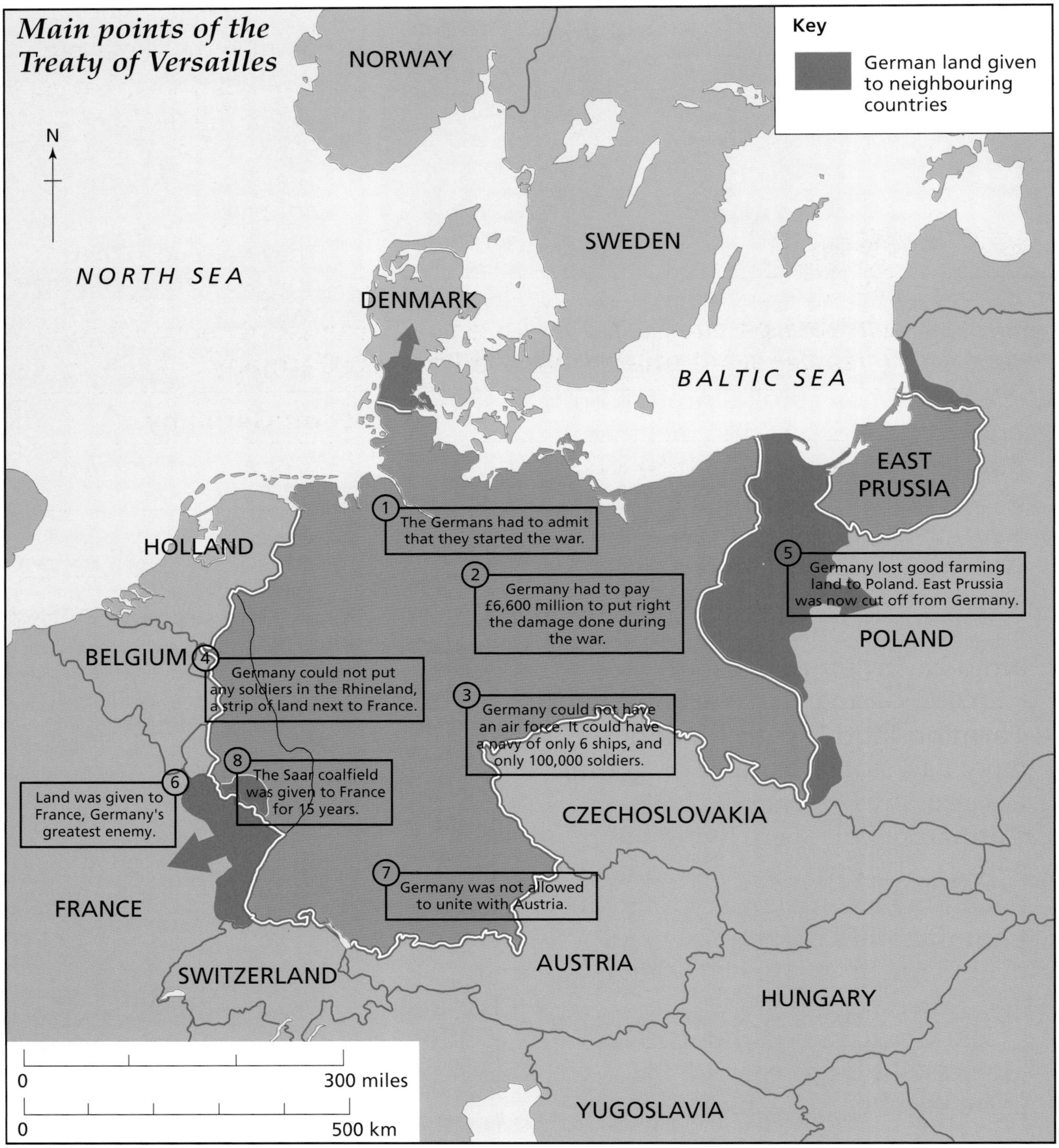

Main points of the Treaty of Versailles
Key
German land given to neighbouring countries
N
NORWAY
SWEDEN
NORTH SEA
DENMARK
BALTIC SEA
EAST PRUSSIA
HOLLAND
BELGIUM
POLAND
CZECHOSLOVAKIA
FRANCE
SWITZERLAND
AUSTRIA
HUNGARY
YUGOSLAVIA
1 The Germans had to admit that they started the war.
2 Germany had to pay £6,600 million to put right the damage done during the war.
3 Germany could not have an air force. It could have a navy of only 6 ships, and only 100,000 soldiers.
4 Germany could not put any soldiers in the Rhineland, a strip of land next to France.
5 Germany lost good farming land to Poland. East Prussia was now cut off from Germany.
6 Land was given to France, Germany's greatest enemy.
7 Germany was not allowed to unite with Austria.
8 The Saar coalfield was given to France for 15 years.
0
300 miles
0
500 km

Germany and the Treaty of Versailles

The Germans only accepted the Treaty because Britain, France and America threatened to go to war again if they did not. Two ordinary Germans – an old soldier and a violin player – had to sign it because no one important in Germany would do so. In Germany a day of public mourning was declared. The Germans hated the Treaty.

Lloyd George, the Prime Minister of Britain, knew that the Germans wanted revenge. He said: 'We will have to fight another war all over again in 25 years'. He was right.

NEW WORDS

Treaty: an agreement between two countries.
threatened, accepted, violin, mourning, revenge
unite
Versailles

The Treaty of Versailles had 200 pages and 75,000 words.

Tasks

1. Working with a partner, suggest for each of the eight terms of the Treaty of Versailles what effect it would have on Germany.

	Effect on Germany
Admit Germany started the war	
Pay for damage done	
Tiny army and navy	
No army in Rhineland	
Farming land lost to Poland	
Land lost to France	
Could not unite with Austria	
Saar coalfield given to France	

2. Prepare a drama, where a number of Germans go to Versailles to try to change the terms of the Treaty of Versailles. Ask your teacher to be Georges Clemenceau, the leader of France. What does he think about the Treaty – can you persuade him to change his mind?

5 THE CHALLENGE OF COMMUNISM

IN THIS CHAPTER YOU WILL LEARN:

- **TWO revolutions that took place in Russia in 1917;**
- **TWO ways Communist propaganda tried to change history.**

NEW WORDS

Communism: the political ideas of Karl Marx.
revolution: when the government is overthrown.
provisional: temporary.
share, wealth

Communism

Karl Marx (1818–83) changed the world. He said that it was wrong that the rich got all the money, but the poor did all the work. He wanted poor people to take power in a revolution. Everything would be shared out equally, and held in common – which is why his new ideas were called 'communism'.

Many people in Russia were very poor. Many of them thought that Marx's ideas were good ideas.

Russia in 1917

The ruler of Russia was called the Tsar. He kept power by using his army and the secret police.

The March Revolution

Russia lost the First World War with Germany. Millions of Russians were killed. At home, there was not enough food.

In March 1917, people rioted. They forced the Tsar to give up the crown. A group of rich middle-class men took over (this was called the Provisional Government).

What Marx said:

The poor do all the work – but the factory owners get all the money. This is wrong.

One day, the workers will unite and throw out the owners.

The workers will set up a new world communist government where everyone will be happy and equal – no one will have more than anyone else.

The November Revolution

The Provisional Government tried to carry on the war. It did nothing to help the poor people.

The poor people of Russia became more angry. They turned to a man called Lenin.

Lenin was a Marxist, and he promised people 'Peace, Bread and Land'. In November 1917 Lenin and the Communists took power. Nobody lifted a finger to save the Provisional Government.

The ruler of Russia in 1917 was Tsar Nicholas II. His wife Alexandra was a granddaughter of Queen Victoria.

SOURCE A

A Communist poster from the 1920s. It says 'red Moscow is the heart of the World Revolution'

Tasks

1. Match the terms 1–7 with the sentences a–g:

1. Karl Marx
2. Communism
3. Tsar Nicholas II
4. Provisional Government
5. Lenin
6. Peace, bread, land
7. First World War

a. Took over the government of Russia, March–November 1917.
b. What Lenin promised the people of Russia in 1917.
c. Invented Communism
d. The ruler of Russia before 1917.
e. Caused problems in Russia.
f. The leader of the Communist November Revolution.
g. The idea that wealth should be shared equally.

2. Use these facts to write ten lines on 'The Russian Revolution of 1917'.

SOURCE B

This Communist picture shows fat factory owners doing nothing whilst people starve.

The fall of the Winter Palace

Your Mission: to plan a film about the November Revolution.

A Hollywood film-maker has just seen the old Russian film *October* (below), and he wants to make a film which tells the story. He has come to you as an historian to help him.

The film-maker likes these events in the film, and he wants to put them into his film if he can.

The Russians used a different calendar to ours. So Lenin's 1917 Revolution – which we call the November Revolution – the Communists called the October Revolution.

▲ 1. Lenin comes to Russia. He stands on a car and gives a speech to his followers.

2. Communist soldiers climb over the gate and attack the Winter Palace, the headquarters of the Provisional Government. ▼

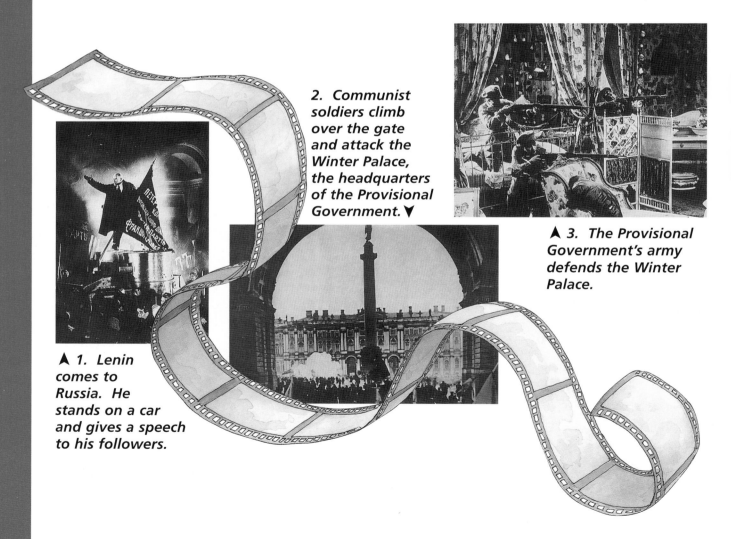

▲ 3. The Provisional Government's army defends the Winter Palace.

SOURCE A

Film of the Winter Palace shows few broken windows, and few bullet-holes in the walls. There was little fighting at the Winter Palace.

Written by a modern historian.

SOURCE C

We all ran up the stairs and into a big hall where the Provisional Government's soldiers were, rifles at the ready.

I was at the front. I shouted, 'Throw down your rifles!' and they did. They saw that we were angry.

A Communist who took part in the attack on the Winter Palace.

SOURCE B

The provisional government was not defeated by a mass attack on the Winter Palace. A few Communists went in by the servants' door and arrested the ministers. Five Communists were shot – by accident by other Communists.

A.J.P. Taylor, a modern historian.

SOURCE D

Lenin came secretly into Russia, so he would not be arrested. He was the leader, but Trotsky (head of the Communist Army) did all the planning.

Written by a modern historian.

SOURCE E

'What happened to the women?' we asked a Communist soldier. 'The women', he laughed. 'We found them hiding in a back room. Some of them were crying – we did not know what to do with them. In the end we just sent them back to their camp.'

Written by an American in Russia at the time.

Tasks

1. Using the Sources, explain to the film-producer why he cannot have the three scenes in his film:

- Lenin gives a speech (see **Source D**);
- Communists storm the Winter Palace (see **Sources A** and **B**);
- The Provisional Government defends the Palace (**Sources C** and **E**).

2. Using the Sources, suggest some good alternative scenes for the film which will be more historically correct.

3. Explain TWO ways in which the Communist government tried to replace history with propaganda. Suggest reasons why it did this.

6 HOW DID COMMUNISM CHANGE RUSSIA?

IN THIS CHAPTER YOU WILL LEARN:

- **THREE things Stalin did to make Russia strong.**

NEW WORDS

difference

noticing

kulak: a wealthy peasant.

collective: a farm made by joining all the villagers' farms together.

terror

opposed

Animal Farm

The book *Animal Farm* was written by the English writer, George Orwell. His story went like this:

Once upon a time there was a farm. It was run by a bad farmer called Mr Jones, who hit and killed the animals. But one day, a pig named Old Major told the animals that they should have a share in the food grown on the farm. He called his ideas 'Animalism'. The animals believed him. Led by the pigs, they drove out Mr Jones.

Soon after, a pig called Napoleon took over the farm. Napoleon told the animals that they must build a windmill, so the farm could have electricity. The animals believed Napoleon, but, although they worked very hard, only the pigs got fatter. Soon after, Napoleon got some dogs, who bit the animals to make them work harder.

One day, the animals crept to the farmhouse window. At the table, they saw Napoleon and the pigs drinking with the local farmers. The animals looked from the pigs to the men, and from the men to the pigs, but they could no longer tell the difference.

SOURCE A

This Communist poster shows a foreigner – who laughs at the 5-Year Plan in 1928 – angry and upset when it succeeds in 1933.

SOURCE B

A mass grave of people shot on Stalin's orders. It was discovered in 1989.

Stalin

In 1924, Stalin took over as leader of Russia. He believed that he had to make Russia strong.

1. More food

Stalin took everybody's farms, and put them together into big farms called collectives. When the *kulaks* (rich peasants) opposed this, seven million *kulaks* were killed.

2. More industry

Stalin made 5-year plans to produce more coal, iron and electricity. People did without food and shoes. Lazy workers who failed to meet targets were shot.

3. Terror

Stalin's secret police (the NKVD) killed anybody who opposed Stalin – about 20 million people in all.

NKVD men who did not shoot enough people were shot!

Tasks

1. Stalin did three things to make Russia strong *(lines 36–51)*. For each, explain how they might have made Russia stronger.

2. Orwell meant *Animal Farm* to be an allegory of the Russian Revolution. Using pages 28–33, say what or who these represented:

the farm – Mr Jones – Old Major – Animalism,
Napoleon – building the windmill – the dogs.

3. Did Orwell think the Russian Revolution had improved things for the Russian people (see *lines 24–31*)?

4. What would the following people have thought about Stalin:

a kulak – a worker – an opponent of Stalin – an NKVD man.

What would they have *said* about Stalin?

Showing the real Joseph Stalin

Your Mission: ***to choose paintings for an exhibition on Stalin.***

It is planned to show a painting of Stalin in the Town Hall. You have been shown three different paintings, but ALL three paintings give an image of Stalin very different from the facts about Stalin.

Stalin is too rude.
He should not be the leader of the Communist Party.
He should be sacked.

What Lenin said about Stalin in 1924.

Painting 1. Lenin comes to Russia in 1917. Stalin was NOT there at the time, but he gave orders that he had to be in the painting.

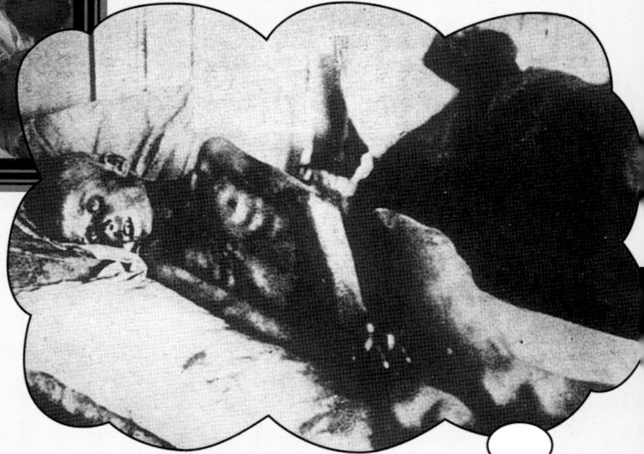

Collective farms did not work. People starved to death.

Painting 2. Stalin on a collective farm.

Painting 3. This painting shows that ordinary people loved Stalin.

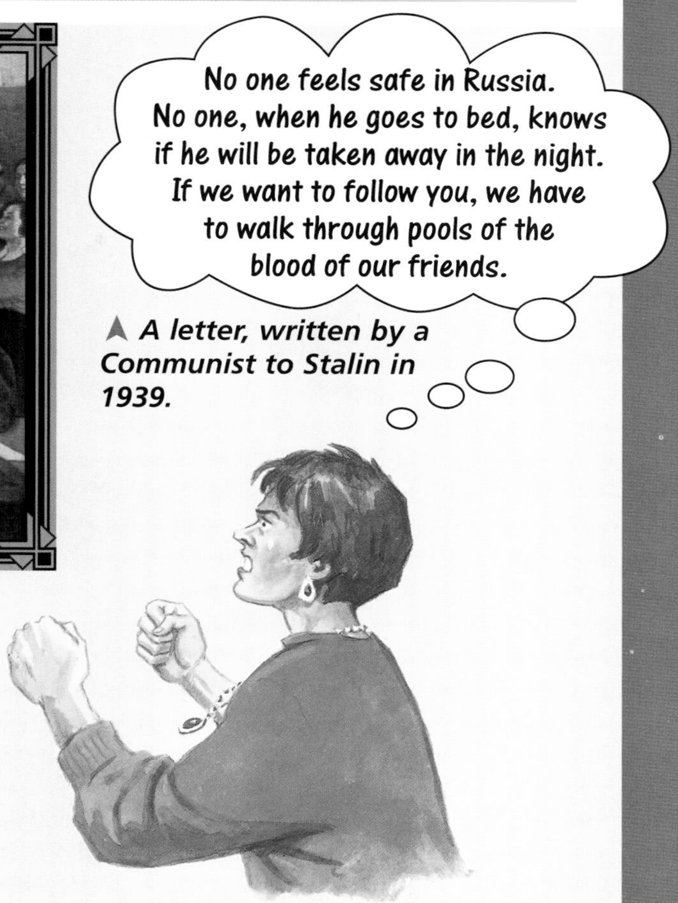

No one feels safe in Russia. No one, when he goes to bed, knows if he will be taken away in the night. If we want to follow you, we have to walk through pools of the blood of our friends.

A letter, written by a Communist to Stalin in 1939.

NEW WORDS

image, photograph, famine

Tasks

1. The pictures show an historian looking at three paintings of Stalin. Each painting reminds her of some historical facts (in the thought bubbles). Working with a partner, discuss how the historical facts contradict the message of the paintings.

2. Ask your teacher to be the exhibition organiser. Explain how NONE of the paintings give a true picture of what Stalin was like.

3. Choose a painting to be in the exhibition. The organiser has asked you to write the programme notes for it.

Do so, explaining:

- what the painting shows,
- how it tries to make Stalin look good,
- what the truth was about Stalin's rule.

7 THE END OF GERMAN DEMOCRACY

IN THIS CHAPTER YOU WILL LEARN:

- **FOUR theories about how Hitler got power;**
- **FOUR good and FOUR bad things about life in Nazi Germany.**

NEW WORDS

economic depression: when factories close and people lose jobs.

Chancellor

describe

Youth

taught

Adolf Hitler

In 1919, after Germany lost World War One, an angry ex-soldier called Adolf Hitler joined a small political party in southern Germany. He became its leader, and changed its name to the Nazi Party.

In 1924, Hitler wrote a book called *Mein Kampf*, in which he set down his ideas. It was full of hatred for the Communists and the Jews who, he said, had made Germany lose the war. German, 'Aryan' people, he wrote, were better than other peoples – they should rule the world. Most of all, Hitler promised to destroy the hated Treaty of Versailles.

SOURCE A

Everything went black. I went back to my bed, put my head into my pillow and cried. The feeling got worse as the days went by. I came to hate the people who did this terrible crime to Germany

▲ ***Hitler, writing about how he felt when he heard that Germany had asked for an Armistice. At the time he was in hospital, blinded by a gas attack.***

SOURCE B

▲ ***Hitler was a great public speaker. Think of words which describe the faces of the listeners in this painting.***

In 1923, Hitler tried to take over Germany by a revolution. It failed, and he was sent to prison.

◄ Adolf Hitler was born in Austria in 1889. He was a mummy's boy, and went off the rails when she died. He ended up living as a tramp.

When World War One started, he joined the German army – he was happy, fighting for the German people. But when Germany lost the war, he was angry, and filled with hate.

The road to power

Hitler set up a youth club, called the Hitler Youth, where children were told these ideas – and taught to love Hitler. He used newspapers and radio to get his ideas across.

The German people liked his ideas (and if people did not agree, Hitler had an army of thugs called 'stormtroopers' who beat them up). But they did not vote for Hitler.

Hitler takes power

Then, in 1929, there was a terrible economic depression in Germany. Six million people were out of a job. The German government could not cope. Some Germans became Communists. Many others started to vote for Hitler and the Nazis. The Nazis became the biggest party in Germany.

In 1933, the President of Germany asked Hitler to help him in the government. He made Hitler the Chancellor. This was what Hitler wanted – he made a law saying that he could make any law he wanted.

Hitler – who had once been a tramp – was now the ruler of Germany!

SOURCE C

▲ Many businessmen were afraid of the Communists (who would take away their businesses if they got into power). They gave money to Hitler to help him get into power.

Task

Which of these ideas best explains Hitler's rise to power:

a. He was a clever man who brilliantly took power.

b. Hitler did not take power – the German people chose him because they wanted what he believed in.

c. Hitler did not take power – the German people chose him because they were desperate.

d. Hitler did not take power – he was given it by a foolish President.

A better life under the Nazis?

The workers

Hitler gave German men work. Many got jobs building the new roads and public buildings. Others got jobs in the armed forces because Hitler started to build up the army and the airforce. Also, when the Nazis came to power, many employers sacked their Jewish workers – German men got their jobs. By 1939, almost every man in Germany had a job.

Trade Unions were banned – instead, German workers had to join the Nazi 'Labour Front'. They were given free picnics and (for a very few people) free holidays – but they were not allowed to go on strike. Men who refused to work were put into concentration camps.

SOURCE A

Most of the men given work by the Nazis worked long hours, in bad conditions, for little more than they got before on the dole.

Written by a modern historian.

Women and girls

Hitler believed that a woman's place was in the home. Girls in the BDM (the Nazi youth club for girls) did cooking and washing up. German girls were taught 'the three Cs' – 'children, church, cooker'. Many women lost their jobs. Instead, women who had more than 8 children were given a medal.

SOURCE B

A poster showing a new road built by the Nazis.

SOURCE C

A poster suggesting that workers could save up and buy a car.

Nazi boys

Most boys in Nazi Germany joined the Hitler Youth. Here, they were prepared to be soldiers in the German army. They went to camp, went marching, and learned how to fire a gun. They were taught to love and obey Hitler.

NEW WORDS

armed forces
concentration camps
suggest, cruel, violent
report, salute

SOURCE D

School children give their teachers the Nazi salute.

SOURCE E

We own him from the cradle to the grave.

We do not let him go until he dies, even if he does not like it.

Said by Dr Robert Ley, head of the Labour Front, about the German workers.

ALL of the six women Hitler went out with during his life either killed themselves, or tried to do so.

The Nazis made sure that all teachers joined the Nazi Party. Teachers had to teach that Jews were bad. They taught Maths – but the sums asked things like how much money would be saved if mental patients were put to death, or how far a shell would go when it was fired from a gun.

German children were taught to be cruel and violent. They were taught that they were part of a new Germany which would conquer the world. And they were told to report their parents to the police if they heard them say anything bad about Hitler.

Tasks

1. Choose to 'be' one of the following – a girl, a boy, a woman or a man – in Nazi Germany. Work with someone else who has chosen the same as you. Using the information on these pages, make a list of FOUR good things about your life in Nazi Germany. Then make a list of FOUR bad things.

2. Discuss as a whole class: 'Was life good under the Nazis?'

How did the Nazis control Germany?

The Nazis tried to control the German people 'from the cradle to the grave'. Firstly, they poured Nazi lies into their heads in every way possible. Secondly, they used terror, so people would not dare to oppose Hitler.

NEW WORDS
propaganda: publicity which sees only the government's side of things.
eternal: everlasting.
accused, disappeared, pure, gypsies, homosexuals, Gestapo

Nazi propaganda

SOURCE A

▲ ***A poster for the film* The Eternal Jew, *which showed Jews as bad people who hated Germany.***

Lie 1:
Jews are not as good as Germans. They are not even human. They made Germany lose World War One. They are cheats who steal your money. They are Communists and want Russia to conquer Germany.

SOURCE B

▲ ***The perfect German family – a Nazi painting.***

Lie 2:
The Germans are the master race who should rule the world. True Germans are blond, with blue eyes and strong bodies. Germans need not obey the same rules as other people.

SOURCE C

▲ ***Hitler speaking at a Nazi rally.***

Lie 3:
Hitler is never wrong. Hitler saved Germany. Hitler cares for the people.

Nazi terror

In Germany it was against the law to oppose Hitler. The secret police – the Gestapo – had spies everywhere. People accused of saying bad things about Hitler were taken away to be 're-educated'. They were put in prison, tortured and killed. Hundreds more simply disappeared – the Gestapo would come at night, there would be lots of shouting, and banging . . . and in the morning your father would be gone. You would never see him again.

Making Germany 'pure'

The Nazis killed more than just their opponents. They wanted to make Germany 'pure' by getting rid of all but the perfect Germans. Jews, gypsies, homosexuals, criminals and tramps were all sent to concentration camps. Patients in mental hospitals were killed.

Most Germans did not agree with this, but it was too dangerous to say anything. Most Germans looked the other way.

SOURCE E

. . . whipping, kicking, slaps in the face, shooting or cutting. Some prisoners were made to stare for hours into bright lights.

▲ *Torture in the concentration camps – this list was written by an historian.*

SOURCE D

▲ ***Members of the Hitler Youth burn books which the Nazis do not like. Onto the fire goes any book written by a Jew or a Communist, all the books which disagree with Nazi ideas, and any book the Nazis think is 'soft' or rude.***

Tasks

1. Using page 40, list THREE methods the Nazis used to get their lies across.

2. Imagine you are a parent in Nazi Germany, trying to explain to your child that the Nazis are wrong. Choose **Source A, B** or **C**. What could you say to show your child that this is wrong?

3. Most Germans 'looked the other way'. Could they have done anything else?

Hitler's War?

***Your Mission:** to produce a report for the British government on Hitler's military intentions.*

It is 1939. You have been asked by the British government to advise them if you think Hitler is going to go to war against Britain. You have done some research and found **Sources A–G** shown here.
What do you think?

SOURCE A

War is the most normal and ordinary thing.
War is everywhere.
There is no such thing as peace. War is life.

▲ *Hitler, writing in* Mein Kampf *in 1924.*

SOURCE B

Germany would give up all its army and all its weapons – if the other countries would do the same.

▲ ***Hitler, speaking in 1933. At this time, Germany was building up its armed forces.***

SOURCE C

1933: 3 **1937: 8** **1939: 37**

▲ ***Germany's spending on its armed forces (in millions of marks).***

SOURCE D

▲ ***A Nazi Sports Day in 1935. Pupils in this race are running in uniforms and gas masks.***

SOURCE E

We will only be safe against Russia if we have an army they are frightened of.

▲ *Hitler, speaking to the British government in 1935.*

SOURCE F

The population of Germany is growing by one million people a year. We need new land for those people to live. By new land, I mean Russia and Poland.

▲ *Hitler, writing in* **Mein Kampf** *in 1924. He wrote this to try to get Germans to vote for him.*

SOURCE G

'Do you want to go to war against Britain and France?' I asked. Hitler looked at me. 'What else do you think we are re-arming for?' he said. 'We must go carefully. I do not know how we are going to do it. But we will win in the end.'

▲ *Written by H. Rauschning, a man who knew Hitler, but hated him. He fled to England, where he wrote this, in 1939. He may have been lying.*

Hitler once showed some French visitors all Germany's airplanes. Then he drove them to another airport. While they were driving there, the German planes flew ahead of them to the airport, so that the visitors would think the Germans had twice as many planes as they did.

Tasks

1. Look at **Sources A** and **F**. Did Hitler say he wanted war in 1924? Do you believe him?

2. Look at **Source B**. Did Hitler say he wanted a strong army in 1933? Do you believe what he said?

3. Sources C and **D** show that Germany was building up a strong army during the 1930s. Does this ***prove*** that Hitler wanted to go to war (look at **Source E**)?

4. Look at **Source G**. Do you think Hitler really wanted to go to war with Britain in 1939, or do you think that Rauschning was just trying to get him into trouble?

5. Answer these questions for the British government, and say which source you think proves your opinion right:

- Does Hitler want Germany to be strong?
- Is Hitler prepared to go to war to get what he wants?
- Is Hitler getting Germany ready for a war if there is one?
- Is Hitler determined to have a war with Britain?
- Is Hitler determined to have a war with Russia?
- Has Hitler wanted war from the very beginning or is he just bluffing?

8 THE SURVIVAL OF DEMOCRACY

IN THIS CHAPTER YOU WILL LEARN:

- **FOUR dictators of the 1930s;**
- **FOUR ways black people tried to get equality after 1920.**

NEW WORDS

democracy: where the people elect their government.
fascists: Nazis.
dictator: a ruler with total power.

Europe of the dictators

In Italy, in 1922, the fascist ruler ***Mussolini*** came to power. After 1933, ***Hitler*** ruled Germany. In Spain, the fascists, led by General ***Franco*** – and after a long civil war – took power in 1939.

In Russia, the Communists took power. After 1924, the dictator ***Stalin*** ruled in Russia.

SOURCE A

The Italian dictator Mussolini. He put money into industry, and gave people jobs. He gave help to poor people. But he also had his opponents shot.

Task

- Use *lines 1–10* to make a table with 4 rows to show 'The Four Dictators', and three columns to show their 'Name', 'Country' and 'Date they came to power'.

The General Strike started because the mine-owners tried to make the coal miners work longer hours for less pay. The coal miners refused to back down when the General Strike ended. The coal strike lasted for 6 months. But, in the end, the miners had to go back to work – for longer hours and less pay.

SOURCE B

In Britain, Oswald Mosley tried to copy Hitler and Mussolini. There were 20,000 fascists in Britain in 1934. They wore black shirts, beat up their opponents, and attacked Jews.

SOURCE C

▲ ***In 1936, 200 men marched from the north-east of England to London. They wanted to show people that they were not out of work because they were lazy.***

Q

- Talk about what you know about our democratic system in Britain today.
- What are the advantages of democracy? Does democracy have any disadvantages?

Democracy in danger

The only important countries which were democracies in the 1930s were America, Britain and France.

In all these countries, there were many people who wanted the country to turn communist. And there were people who wanted a fascist dictator like Hitler.

Britain 1919–1939

During the First World War, the government had promised people jobs and better houses. After the war, it broke its promises. It said it could not pay for these things.

British businesses closed down – mainly in the coal, steel and ship-building industries. Many British people were poor and out of work.

In 1926, many workers went on strike – there was a 'General Strike' for 9 days. Some people thought that it was the start of a Communist rebellion in Britain.

SOURCE D

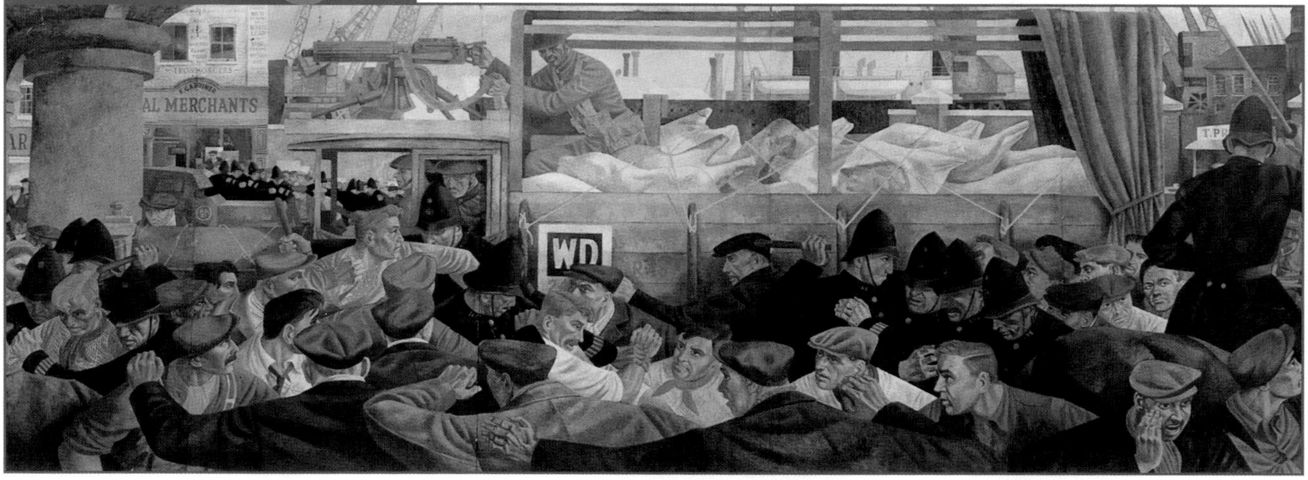

▲ ***This painting shows workers fighting with police in the 1926 General Strike. In fact, the General Strike was mostly a peaceful strike.***

SOURCE E

▲ ***Not everyone was poor in the 1930s. There were many new gadgets for the home. Partly, this was because people could no longer afford to pay servants.***

The Depression

In America in the 1920s, businessmen invented hire purchase – getting something now, but paying for it a bit at a time over the next few months. This let people buy more things, and the American economy boomed.

Then, in 1929, the American economy fell apart. It happened so quickly that it was called 'the Crash'. Banks went bankrupt, factories closed down. Millions lost their jobs:

Once I built a railroad, made it run,
Made it race against time.
Once I built a railroad, now it's gone –
Buddy can you spare a dime?

Once I built a tower, to the sun,
Brick and iron and lime.
Once I built a tower, now it's gone –
Buddy can you spare a dime?

Q

- What is the song-writer having to do to live, now he has lost his job?

SOURCE F

NEW WORDS

Hire purchase: buying things on credit.
Economy: the world of business – banks, factories and shops.
spare, gadgets, pensions

◄ ***These men want to work so much that they say they will work for just $1 a week.***

The New Deal

By 1932, there were more than 12 million Americans out of work. Some people starved to death. Millions were homeless.

In 1932, many jobless people set up a shanty town in Washington. The government used the army to drive them away – it looked as though democracy was in danger even in America.

Then, in 1932, Franklin D. Roosevelt became President. He promised the American people a 'New Deal'. The government spent lots of money to make jobs for people building schools, playgrounds and dams. It gave pensions to old people, and unemployment pay to people out of work. It helped people who had got into money problems.

SOURCE G

An American poster from 1941. The Depression only really ended when countries began to get ready for war in the late 1930s.

Tasks

Answer the following questions.

1. Why was democracy in danger in the 1930s (*lines 11–19*)?

2. Which industries were worst-hit in the Depression (*lines 26–28*)?

3. Find TWO reasons people in Britain were angry (page 45).

4. What event made many people in Britain think their democracy was in danger (*lines 30–34*)?

5. Why did the American economy boom in the 1920s (*lines 36–40*)?

6. What was 'the Crash' (*lines 41–44*)?

7. What were the effects of the Depression in America (*lines 54–57*)?

8. What event made many Americans think their democracy was in danger (*lines 58–63*)?

9. How did Roosevelt give Americans a 'New Deal' (*lines 64–73*)?

10. What ended the Depression (**Source G**)?

Black Americans between the wars

Racism in the USA

Slavery was abolished in America in 1865, but black people were still kept in badly-paid jobs.

NEW WORDS

lynched: hanged by a mob.
NAACP: National Association for the Advancement of Colored People.
boycott: refuse to use.
units, cinema

SOURCE A

"Liberty And Freedom Shall Not Perish"
A. Lincoln
COLORED MEN The First Americans Who Planted Our Flag on the Firing Line
TRUE SONS OF FREEDOM

This picture shows black soldiers fighting in World War One, while Abraham Lincoln – who abolished slavery – looks on. The first US soldier to win a medal was black – but when the black soldiers came back, they found that nothing had changed.

Many American states passed 'Jim Crow' laws which stopped blacks using the same schools, buses and swimming baths as white people. In the south, the Ku Klux Klan led race hatred against the blacks. Klan members put on white robes and hoods. They attacked blacks, Jews, Communists and Catholics.

SOURCE B

Thousands of black soldiers fought for America in the First World War, but they were still treated badly. The navy would only let blacks be cooks. The army took black soldiers, but it kept them in blacks-only units, and gave them white officers.

A modern historian.

SOURCE C

In 1919, white mobs rioted through the black areas of Chicago. Earlier that day, a drowning black man clinging to a log drifted into a 'whites only' swimming area in Chicago. It was the start of 2 years of race riots.

The blacks fight back

In 1909, the NAACP was formed. It held ***Silent Marches*** to protest about the way blacks were treated.

In the 1920s, black people became writers, poets, film stars and dancers. It was in the 1920s that black people first began to say: 'Black is beautiful'. They called this ***'artistic action'*** to get equality.

In the 1930s, blacks did other things to get equality. They ***boycotted*** shops which did not employ black people. And they ***voted for Roosevelt*** – when he came to power, black people were helped by the New Deal.

But when America entered World War Two in 1941, blacks were still the poorest people in America, and they still did not have equal rights with whites.

In 1925, the US Senate threw out a bill which tried to make lynchings illegal.

SOURCE **E**

A 1920s jazz band – black people invented jazz music in 1917. Many white people liked jazz, but others said it would harm young people.

SOURCE **D**

A cinema with different doors for blacks and whites. Signs like this became common after 1919.

Tasks

1. Using pages 48–49, find all the ways in which blacks were discriminated against.

2. Why would black soldiers have been angered by the scenes in **Sources C** and **D**?

3. List the ***FOUR ways*** blacks campaigned for equality after 1920. How did these methods hope to get equality for black people? Did they work?

Why was Nancy Astor important?

***Your Mission:** to publicise the importance of Nancy Astor.*

Nancy Astor, 1879–1964.

SOURCE A

Nancy Astor changed the man's world of Parliament. Never again could men think only about what men wanted. She changed everything.

A modern woman historian.

Nancy Astor

In 1918, after the First World War, women were given the vote. In the elections the next year, 1919, the first woman MP took her seat in Parliament.

Nancy Astor was the daughter of an American millionaire, but she had married an Englishman. She had never been a suffragette, and she took over her husband's safe seat in Plymouth when he was made a lord.

Lady Astor was forceful and cheeky – 'I am the kind of woman I would run away from,' she once said. About women's rights, she said, 'We don't want to be better than men – we are that already. We just want to be equal.'

When Lady Astor went to Parliament, they had to change the toilets – but did she change anything else . . .

Winston Churchill and Nancy Astor hated each other. Once, Lady Astor said to him: 'If you were my husband, I would poison your coffee!' Churchill replied: 'And if you were my wife, madam, I would drink it'.

NEW WORDS

married, maternity
fair, chance

SOURCE B

It is sometimes said that the small band of women MPs did not do much.

This is not true. In the 1920s there were 16 Acts of Parliament which helped women, mostly to do with maternity hospitals and making divorce fairer.

A modern woman historian.

SOURCE C

Nancy Astor was the first woman MP. Since that time, there have never been many women MPs in Parliament, usually about 20, and it is hard to find anything they have done.

A modern school textbook, written in 1970.

SOURCE D

Young women on their way to vote in 1929.

SOURCE E

1. Milk for poor children.
2. Help for unmarried mothers.
3. Job training for women.
4. Child abuse.
5. Women police.

A list of the things Lady Astor spoke about in Parliament.

SOURCE F

Most women MPs in the 1920s tried to make women's lives better as 'wives and mothers'. They did not try to get them real equality, power or the chance of a good career.

A modern woman historian.

Task

You want people in Plymouth to vote for Nancy Astor again, so you go canvassing from door to door. What will you tell people about:

- what she has done for women;
- how she has changed Parliament;
- why we must have women MPs.

Sources A–F will give you ideas of what to say.

Once, Churchill tried to speak in Parliament when he had drunk too much. A woman M.P. told him, 'Sir, you are drunk.' Churchill replied, 'And you, madam, are ugly. But I shall be sober tomorrow.'

9 WORLD WAR TWO 1939–42

IN THIS CHAPTER YOU WILL LEARN:

- FOUR reasons France fell;
- THREE bad things about the Blitz.

NEW WORDS

Prime Minister
determination
French Resistance: people who fought the Nazis behind the lines.
Luftwaffe: German air force.

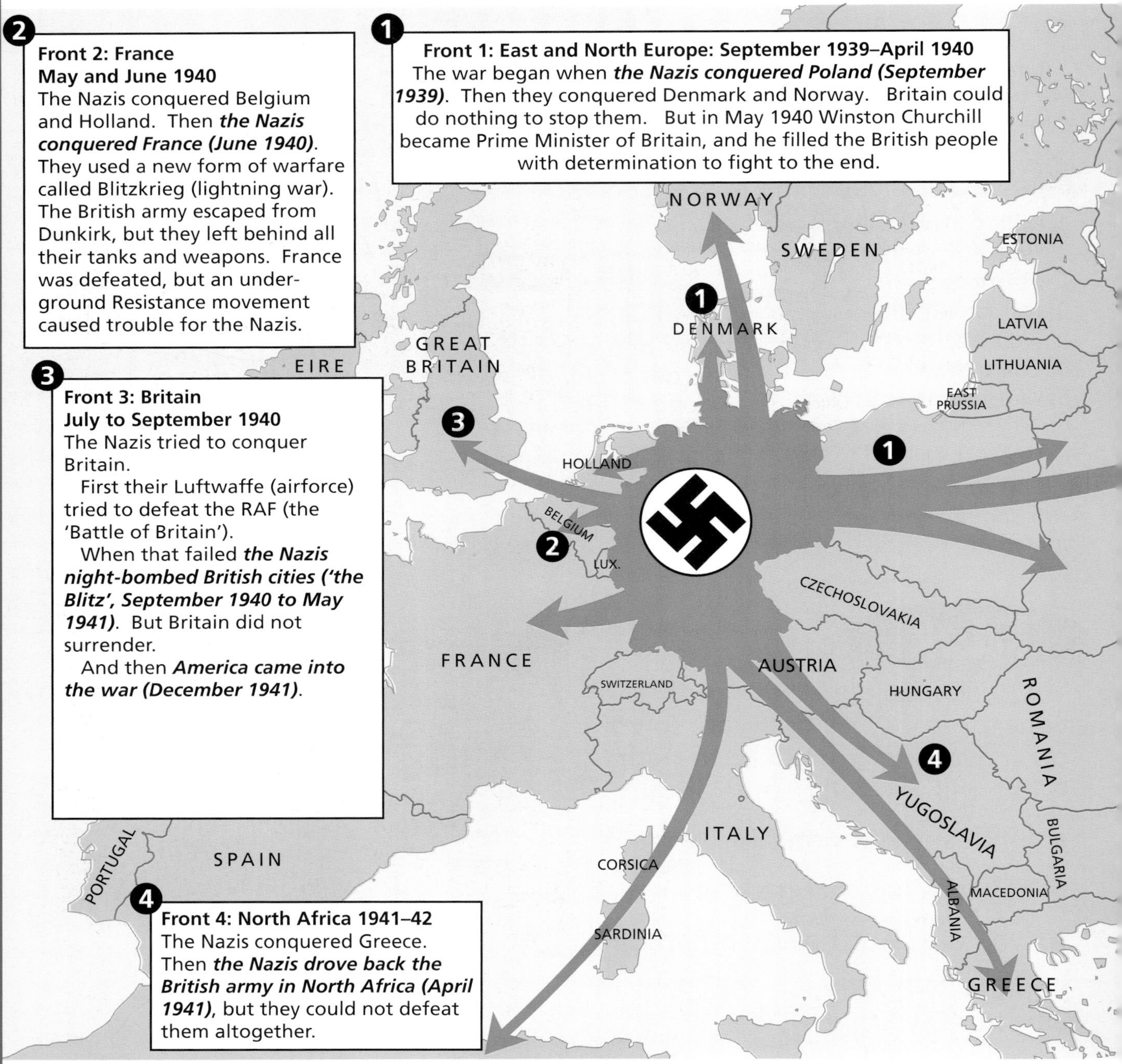

1 Front 1: East and North Europe: September 1939–April 1940
The war began when ***the Nazis conquered Poland (September 1939)***. Then they conquered Denmark and Norway. Britain could do nothing to stop them. But in May 1940 Winston Churchill became Prime Minister of Britain, and he filled the British people with determination to fight to the end.

2 Front 2: France
May and June 1940
The Nazis conquered Belgium and Holland. Then ***the Nazis conquered France (June 1940)***. They used a new form of warfare called Blitzkrieg (lightning war). The British army escaped from Dunkirk, but they left behind all their tanks and weapons. France was defeated, but an underground Resistance movement caused trouble for the Nazis.

3 Front 3: Britain
July to September 1940
The Nazis tried to conquer Britain.
First their Luftwaffe (airforce) tried to defeat the RAF (the 'Battle of Britain').
When that failed ***the Nazis night-bombed British cities ('the Blitz', September 1940 to May 1941)***. But Britain did not surrender.
And then ***America came into the war (December 1941)***.

4 Front 4: North Africa 1941–42
The Nazis conquered Greece. Then ***the Nazis drove back the British army in North Africa (April 1941)***, but they could not defeat them altogether.

Tasks

Imagine you are one of Hitler's generals, making a report on the state of the war in 1942.

1. List all the successes that the German armies have had since 1939.

2. On all five fronts, however, dangers remain. Explain them to your listeners.

3. Looking to the next 3 years, do you think the Nazis are going to win the war:

- easily
- with difficulty
- not at all – they will lose it.

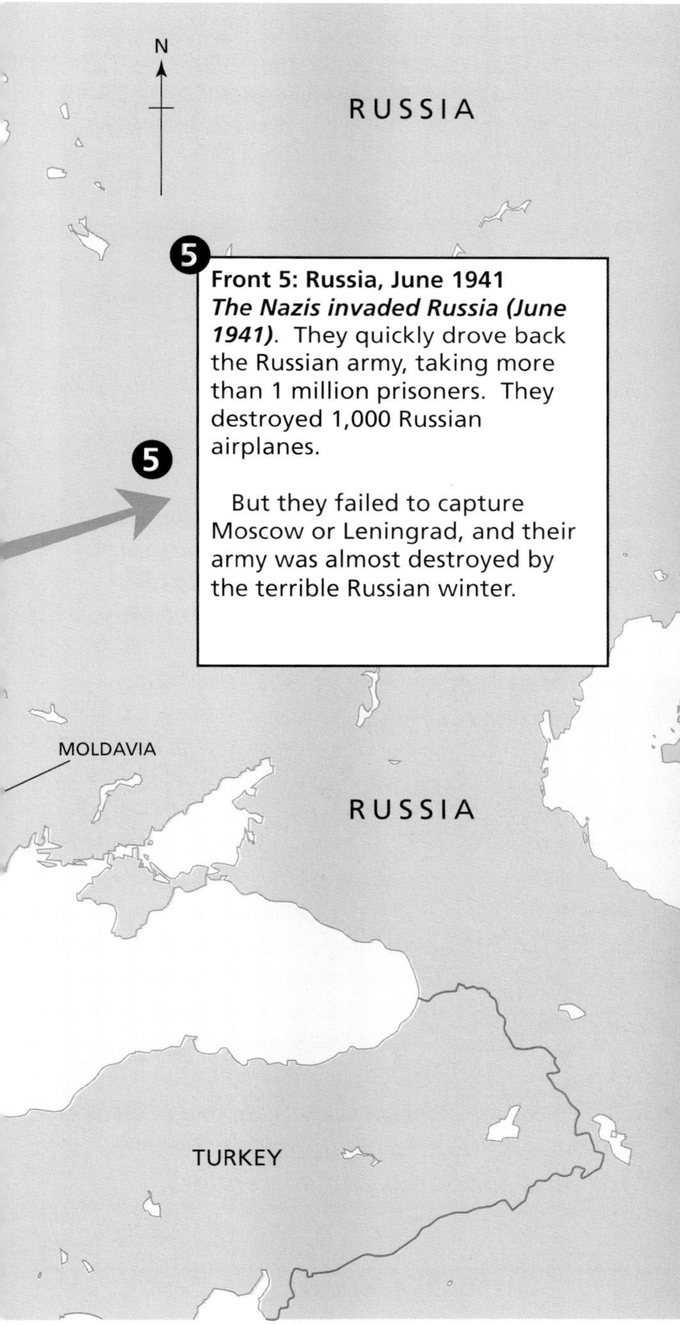

5 **Front 5: Russia, June 1941**

The Nazis invaded Russia (June 1941). They quickly drove back the Russian army, taking more than 1 million prisoners. They destroyed 1,000 Russian airplanes.

But they failed to capture Moscow or Leningrad, and their army was almost destroyed by the terrible Russian winter.

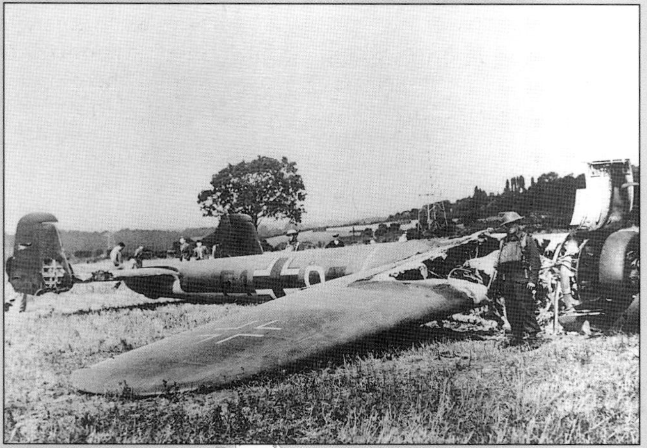

Picture 1 *A German fighter plane shot down in the south of England.*

Picture 2 *Russians murdered by the Nazis.*

Why was Blitzkrieg so successful?

France's defences

After World War One, the French were determined that France would never be invaded again. They built a strong super-trench, called the Maginot Line, along their border with Germany. The French in the miles of underground tunnels and forts thought they could not be beaten – 'They shall not pass', was the motto of the soldiers.

Surprisingly, the Maginot Line only went as far as Belgium, where it stopped. The Nazis, who attacked through Belgium, just went round it.

NEW WORDS

telephone exchanges
paratroopers
chaos

SOURCE A

1. Airplanes bomb the troops, and all the army headquarters, bridges, roads and telephone exchanges behind the enemy front line.

2. Paratroopers and gliders land behind the enemy front line and cause chaos, capturing important bridges and buildings.

3. Groups of tanks, called Panzer units, attack the weakest part of the enemy line. Then they push far into the enemy, followed by soldiers in trucks.

4. The enemy's front line finds itself cut off from its supports, and surrenders.

How **Blitzkrieg** *works.* *From modern comics.*

France falls

The Nazi forces swept into north-eastern France on 15 May 1940. They met only a small French army, because the French generals had thought the land was too hilly for the Nazi tanks.

The French and British armies panicked. By 22 May, the British generals were making plans to take their troops home from Dunkirk.

The Nazis overran the Allied armies. On 28 May Belgium surrendered. By 14 June the Nazis had got to Paris. The French general Pétain surrendered, on 22 June. The Nazis took over all the north of France, leaving Pétain in control of a Nazi state in the south.

It took the Nazis only 7 weeks to conquer France. They lost only 30,000 men killed or wounded in the entire campaign.

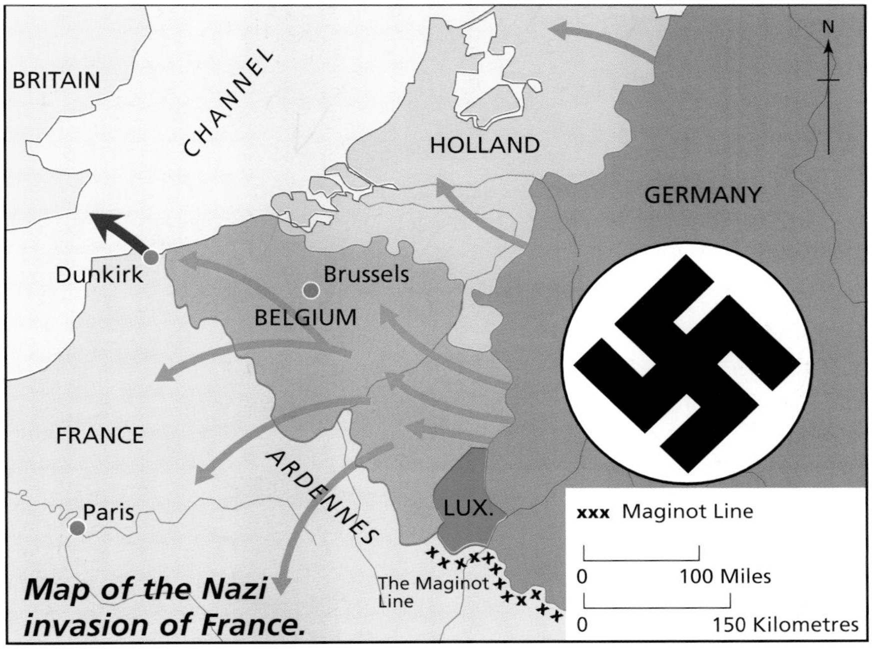

Map of the Nazi invasion of France.

SOURCE B

The battle of France was not won because the Nazi army was bigger. The French had more tanks than the Nazis. But in their tactics, and in their leaders, the Nazis outclassed the British and French.

Written by a modern historian.

SOURCE C

Love of fun was stronger than the spirit of duty. People said what they wanted, not what they could give. They were lazy, and so the bad times have come.

Said by Pétain in 1940 about the French people.

Tasks

1. The pictures in **Source A** are from comics. Are they useless to a professional historian?

2. Study **Source C**. Why did Pétain think that France had been defeated?

3. Look through the text on pages 54–55. Can you find FOUR other possible reasons for the fall of France?

4. What do YOU think was the main reason for the fall of France.

How did people get through the Blitz?

Your Mission: to prepare a propaganda leaflet about the Blitz.

65,000 British and 600,000 German civilians were killed by bombing between 1939 and 1945.

The Blitz

For 76 nights, the Nazis bombed London. Many people were killed or badly hurt. About $1\frac{1}{2}$ million were made homeless. Many other British cities were bombed.

Winston Churchill said on the radio that Londoners were pleased to be sharing the horrors of war with the British soldiers. It was only partly true. In some places people were ready to give up.

SOURCE A

People sheltering in a tube station. About 160,000 Londoners slept in the tube every night to get away from the bombs.

SOURCE B

The first time I went there I felt sick. I had to come out. The smell was terrible.

There were thousands of people lying head to toe underneath the arches.

And there were only four buckets at the far end for toilets.

People sleeping under the railway arches in London. Written by a person at the time.

SOURCE C

$1\frac{1}{2}$ million families were given Anderson shelters, which they put in their back gardens. They could not stand up to being hit by a bomb.

SOURCE D

It felt good when I had got a body ready to be buried, but I could not use too many body parts, or another body would have sad gaps.

And then there were always spare arms or legs.

A woman, talking about her job getting bomb victims ready to be buried.

When war broke out, the government made 1 million coffins. But because they needed wood for the war, they made them out of papier mâché.

SOURCE E

We left the shelter and went home.

There was no home. All that was left was a pile of bricks.

We had nowhere to live. For 6 months we had to live in the shelter.

What happened to one Liverpool family.

SOURCE F

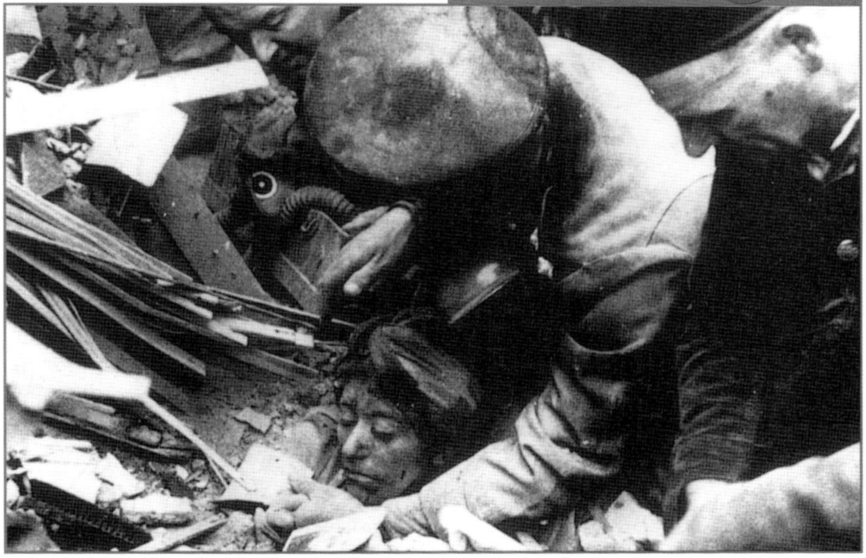

A woman is pulled – alive! – from her bombed house.

SOURCE G

The morning after – finding out who had died.

Tasks

1. Using pages 56–57, find THREE bad things about the Blitz.

Write a leaflet to answer:

- Are we all going to die?
- What happens if I die?
- Is there anywhere nice to shelter?

The government wants you to tell the truth, but to give people hope.

2. Finish with a final paragraph in which you fill people with determination and promise them revenge.

10 WORLD WAR TWO 1942–45

IN THIS CHAPTER YOU WILL LEARN:

- **THIRTEEN key dates of World War Two;**
- **SIX reasons the Nazis lost the Battle of Stalingrad.**

NEW WORDS

invasions

An American bomber over Germany. The wing has been taken off by a bomb dropped from a plane above.

1

1000 Bomber Raids 1942 to 1945
The Nazi Luftwaffe was destroyed.

British and American airplanes bombed German factories, but they also destroyed whole cities.

Dresden was destroyed (14 February 1945). Thousands of Germans were killed.

2

D-Day June 1944 to May 1945
Thousands of British and American soldiers invaded Normandy in France in ***the D-Day invasions (6 June 1944)***. Then they fought their way to Berlin.

Everywhere the troops were greeted like heroes. ***The Allied troops met up with the Russians coming from the east (23 April 1945)***.

In the end, ***Germany surrendered (7 May 1945)***.

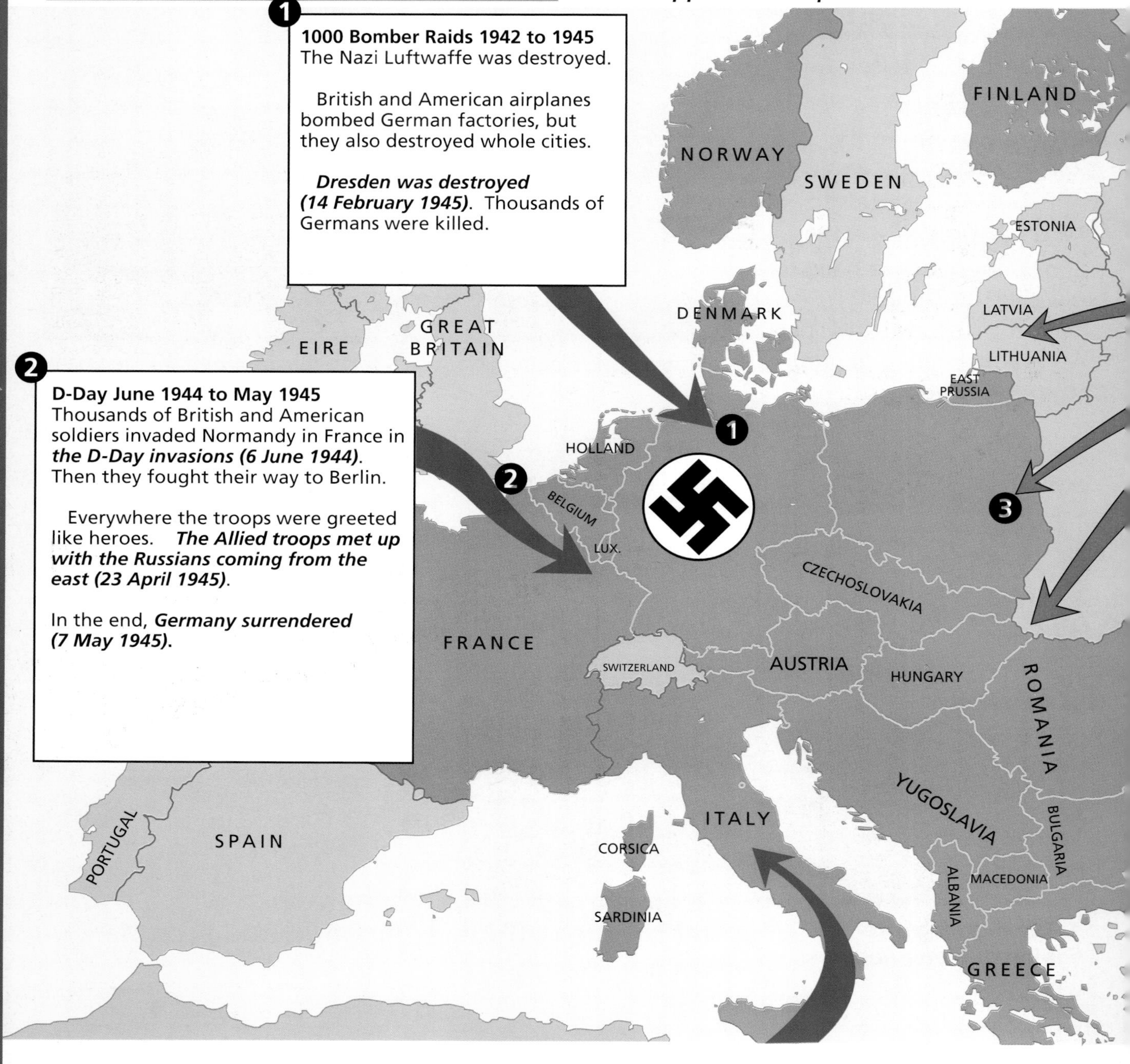

Tasks

1. Copy the ***six dates*** in italics on pages 52–53, and the ***seven dates*** in italics on these pages, and list them in chronological order.

2. Look at your list. What was the turning point of the war?

3. 'Before 1942, we never won. After 1942, we never lost.' Do you agree with this old person's memory of the war?

4. Use pages 52–53 and pages 58–59 to write an account, in no more than 100 words, of the story of World War Two.

5. Look at your story. Now write it in 50 words.

3

The Russian Front – November 1942 to April 1945
After a vast battle, ***the Russians destroyed the Nazi 6th Army at the Battle of Stalingrad (1942–1943)***. Then they slowly pushed back the Nazis.

In the end, ***the Russians took Berlin (2 May 1945)***. When he knew he was going to lose, ***Hitler shot himself (30 April 1945)***.

German prisoners in Russia, 1943.

Gliders were used to drop men behind the Nazi lines.

The end of the Soviet Union?

NEW WORDS

key, surrounded, awesome

Invade!

In June 1942, Hitler told his armies to attack Russia. The Nazis had invaded Russia the year before, but their army had been destroyed by the Russian winter. Now Hitler wanted to cut Russia in half by taking the key town of Stalingrad.

Stalingrad

At first it seemed as if the Nazis would win. They smashed through the Russian army. Everywhere they captured, they killed hundreds of local people. Still the Russians fell back. On 25 August, the Nazi 6th Army reached Stalingrad.

But this time, the Russians did not fall back. They defended every building to the death. A Russian soldier pulled back only when the ground was on fire under him.

One such place in Stalingrad was the Grain Tower. It took the Nazis 2 weeks to take it. When they got in, they found the bodies of just 40 Russians.

SOURCE A

▲ ***A Russian poster asking for men to fight the Nazis.***

SOURCE B

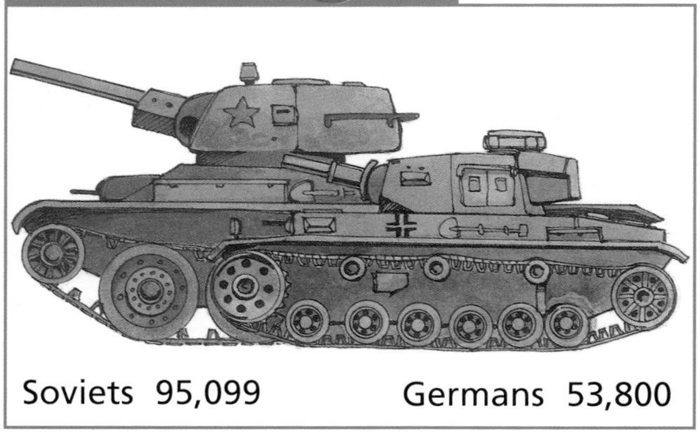

▲ ***Russian and Nazi tank production, 1941–45.***

SOURCE C

A painting from 1948 showing Stalin planning an attack. ▼

And at night – when the dogs jumped into the river and swam for their lives – the Russians took more soldiers into the town.

But the Russians used only enough men to stop the Nazis taking Stalingrad. Secretly, they were collecting millions of men and thousands of tanks behind the lines.

Attack!

On 20 November 1942, the Russians struck. They surrounded the Nazi army and cut it off from the rest of the Nazi forces.

Now it was the Germans' turn to be heroes. For 2 months they held out, waiting for Hitler to send an army to save them. The Russian winter swept in again. Still the Germans held out. No army came.

The Germans had no food, and no bullets. On 31 January 1943, they had to surrender. The defeat was total. More than ¼ million men had invaded – but only 6,000 lived to get back to Germany after the war.

The battle of Stalingrad was awesome. At Stalingrad, the greatest armies the world had ever known smashed into each other in a fight to the death. And the Russians won . . .

Tasks

1. What does **Source A** tell us about how the Russians felt about the Nazis?

2. Look at **Source C.** Who, according to Russian propaganda, won the Battle of Stalingrad.

3. Think through what happened in the story. Can you find SIX other reasons why the Russians won?

4. Write out your list of reasons in order of importance.

On Christmas Day, 1942, Russian radio broadcast a ticking clock. Every 7 seconds, it told the Germans, a German soldier dies.

SOURCE **D**

'Stalin as War Leader' – a painting from the 1980s showing Stalin sweeping Russian soldiers to their deaths.

D-Day

Your Mission: to understand what it was like to land on the Normandy beaches on D-Day.

NEW WORDS

- church services
- truth
- Colonel

D-Day

On 6 June 1944, Allied soldiers landed on five beaches in Normandy. At Omaha beach, the Nazis fought strongly, and 2,400 Americans died in the attack. What was it like to attack the Nazis on that important day?

Stage 1: *The night before*

Some people played cards. Some read books. Some prayed. A Catholic priest held 3 church services – a Catholic, a Protestant and a Jewish one. I went to all three. He asked me, 'What religion are you?' I told him, 'Whatever works.'

Bob Edlin.

Stage 2: *Sailing there*

The seas were more than 2 metres high. The men were so sea-sick they did not care if they lived or died. They were too sick to be scared. After about five miles, they started to feel better.

William Ryan.

Stage 3: *First moments*

I jumped into the water. It was up to my neck. There were bullets pinging into the water near me. I got to the beach and lay down next to the officer. He said, 'What are you doing?' and I said 'Same thing as you, sir.'

John Dandker.

***Soldiers lying on the beach. A picture from the modern film* Saving Private Ryan.**

Stage 4: *Pinned Down*

We realised that we were in a Nazi killing zone of machine-gun fire and shells.

All around me there was chaos – bodies, guns, and everything from socks to toothbrushes.

▲ ***Charles Cawton.***

Stage 5: Going up the beach

We could not move. In the end the ships came in close and shelled the German guns from the sea. I think that is the only reason we won that day.

▲ ***William Ryan.***

The only people who will be left on this beach at the end of today will be the dead ones – so let's get the hell out of here!

▲ ***Colonel Taylor***

Stage 6: *Afterwards*

Our officer was carried back. He had no legs. He asked the doctor if he was going to live. He said, 'Tell me the truth. If I've got a chance, I will stay awake, I will fight. If I have not, I will go to sleep.' I often wonder if he lived. There were so many heroes that day, they could not make enough medals to go round.

▲ ***John Hamilton.***

Tasks

1. Study pages 62–63 and answer the questions. Remember to explain your answers, using evidence from the sources.

a. How did the soldiers feel the night before the invasion?

b. Why were the soldiers not scared as they were sailing there?

c. What made the first moments of the landing so terrifying?

d. What did the soldiers realise when they were pinned down?

e. What allowed the soldiers to go up the beach?

f. How did the soldiers feel afterwards?

Pretend you are an American soldier. Write an imaginary letter home telling your family what happened – and how you felt about it all – on the D-Day landings, 6 June 1944.

11 THE FIRST NUCLEAR WAR

IN THIS CHAPTER YOU WILL LEARN:

- **FOUR facts about the atomic bomb.**

NEW WORDS

kamikaze: Japanese suicide pilots.

centre, shadows

immediately, radiation

worst, guards, acid

After the war, his country destroyed, thousands dead or dying, the Emperor of Japan went on the radio and said: 'The war has not gone quite as we would have wished.'

SOURCE A

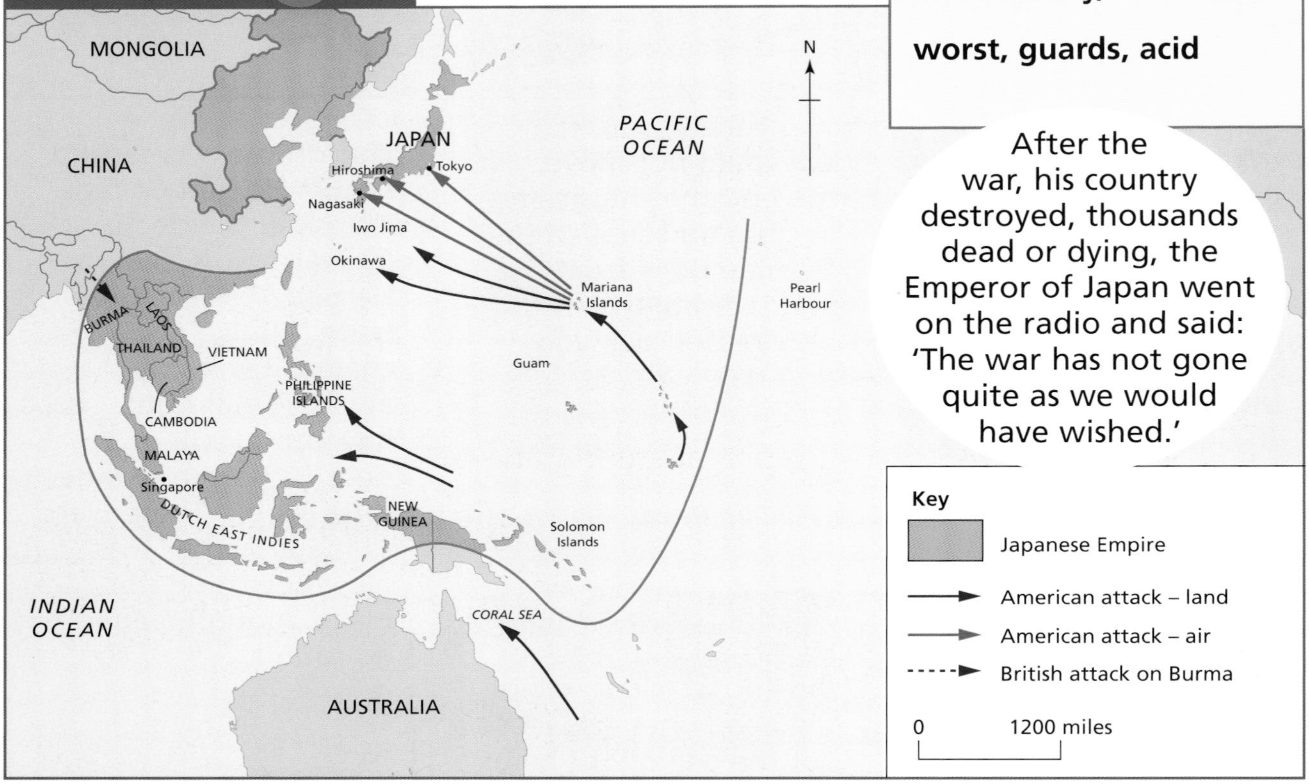

The war in the Far East

Hiroshima

At 2.45 am on 6 August 1945, an American B-29 bomber took off and flew towards Japan. By 8.15 am it was over the town of Hiroshima. Forty-five seconds later there was a blinding light. Then there was a short burst of heat so great that roof tiles melted, and trees and flesh were burned $2\frac{1}{2}$ miles away. People in the town centre were burned so fast that all that was left of them was their shadows, burned into the pavement. Finally, the blast shot outwards at 500 miles an hour, flattening everything for 2 miles around and killing 100,000 people.

SOURCE B

Your trench must be your grave. But before you die, it is your duty to kill ten of the enemy.

An order to Japanese soldiers.

The Americans had dropped the first atomic bomb on Hiroshima. Three days later, the Americans dropped a second atomic bomb – this time on the town of Nagasaki. Again, it destroyed everything.

The war in the East

Japan started the war in December 1941, by making a surprise attack on the American fleet in Pearl Harbor. By 1942, they had conquered most of the Far East.

The Japanese treated the conquered peoples cruelly. Japanese prisoner of war (PoW) camps were the worst in the world.

The British and Americans drove the Japanese soldiers back, but only slowly. The Japanese were fanatics, and they fought to the death. 'Kamikaze' pilots filled their planes with explosives and used themselves as a living bomb.

In May 1945, Germany surrendered. People in Britain and America wanted to stop fighting too. They were told that to invade Japan would cost millions of soldiers' lives – so two atomic bombs were dropped to force Japan to stop. It worked. On 14 August, Japan surrendered.

SOURCE D

The men were ill from having to eat grass and rice and from the dirty conditions.

But the guards kept sick men working for up to 18 hours a day.

▲ *A Japanese Prisoner of War camp. The Japanese did medical experiments on PoWs, injecting them with acid or diseases, or killing them with X-rays.*

In the 1970s there were Japanese soldiers on islands who still refused to surrender although the war had been over for 30 years!

SOURCE C

▲ *An American magazine from during the war with Japan.*

Tasks

1. Look at **Source C**. What did American people think about the Japanese?

2. List FOUR facts about the atomic bomb (page 64).

3. Make a short radio news bulletin such as might have been made on 6 August 1945 by an American radio station. Include:

- facts about the events and details of times, dates etc.;
- why the bomb was dropped;
- the effects of the bomb.

Why did the USA drop the bomb?

Your Mission: to take part in a debate: 'Was the atomic bomb justified?'

Should the A-Bomb have been dropped? Even at the time, when President Truman of the United States used the atomic bomb, not everyone thought that he was right …

SOURCE A

This is a short-cut to end the killing in the east. We can end the war and bring peace to the world, by showing our power at the cost of a few explosions.

Said by Winston Churchill in 1945.

An American poster. Many Americans agreed with the atomic bomb because the Japanese had started the war.

SOURCE B

THE HISTORY OF THE ATOMIC BOMB

1895 Marie Curie discovered radiation.

1919 A British scientist split the atom.

1939 Albert Einstein said an atomic bomb was possible. He told the Allies to make one before the Nazis did.

1940 Two German scientists, who had fled from Nazi Germany, offered to make an atomic bomb for the British.

1942 The Nazis were building an atomic bomb, using what they called 'heavy water'. The Allies bombed the factory.

1942 The US set up the Manhattan Project to make an atomic bomb. British scientists went to help.

1943 A factory to make an atomic bomb was built at Oak Ridge, USA.

16 July 1945 An atomic bomb was tested.

31 July 1945 President Truman ordered the atomic bomb to be used.

6 Aug 1945 Hiroshima

9 Aug 1945 Nagasaki

14 August 1945 Japan surrendered.

SOURCE C

People blinded and burned. 100,000 dead at the time. For years after, babies born deformed, and long, slow deaths from cancer.

Written by a modern historian.

SOURCE D

President Truman wanted to use the bomb to end the war quickly, before the Russians could send their armies in, so that America would have more power in the area.

Written by a military historian.

SOURCE E

There was less and less food. Even the soldiers did not have enough to eat. Winter was coming. I told the emperor that millions of people would die a dog's death from hunger or cold.

Said by a Japanese man. American ships had cut off all trade to Japan, and it was only a matter of time before Japan ran out of everything – such as food, petrol and steel.

SOURCE F

It did not help us beat Japan – Japan was already beaten. They wanted to drop the bomb because they had spent so much money making it.

It was an evil weapon – I did not want to make war that way.

Said by an American admiral in 1945.

SOURCE G

It would have the same effect if we showed them what it could do by exploding it in public in a desert or on a small island.

In 1945, the scientists who made the bomb said that they did not want it to be used. They suggested this other idea.

In the USA during the war, 1 in 8 Americans thought that EVERY Japanese person should be killed.

Tasks

1. Split into two groups.

One group of pupils studies page 66. They use the information to work out all the arguments which suggest America SHOULD have dropped the atomic bomb.

The other group uses page 67 to work out all the arguments that America need not or should not have dropped the bomb.

2. Split into twos. Have an argument. Should the bomb have been dropped?

3. Come together as a whole class. Who won the argument? Take a vote as a whole class – should the bomb have been dropped?

4. It is July 1945. Write a letter or draw a poster for or against the atomic bomb.

12 THE NAZIS AND THE JEWS

IN THIS CHAPTER YOU WILL LEARN:

- **EIGHT steps to the Final Solution.**

NEW WORDS

persecute (persecution): to attack a person for who they are.

human rights

synagogues: Jewish places of worship.

citizen: a person with rights in a country.

final solution: the Nazi attempt to gas all the Jews.

SOURCE A

An illustration from a children's book showing Jewish children and teachers being thrown out of school.

The start

When Hitler came to power in ***1933***,the Nazis started to persecute the Jews. Nazi thugs stood outside Jewish shops to stop people going in. Germans sacked Jewish workers, and stopped going to Jewish doctors.

In school, German children were taught to hate the Jews. Jewish children were put at the front of the class so that everyone could mock them.

Things get worse

During the ***summer of 1935***, signs went up all over Germany: 'Jews not wanted here'. And in ***September 1935***, Hitler passed the Nuremberg Laws. Jews lost many human rights (see **Source B**).

In ***1936***, the Nazis began to try to get Jews to leave Germany. And they began to send some Jews to concentration camps.

The first attacks

Then, in ***1938***, a Jew in France killed a German. All over Germany mobs led by Nazis burned Jewish shops and synagogues. Thousands of Jews were beaten up or taken away. The night was called *Kristallnacht* – glass night – because of all the windows the Nazis broke.

During the war

The Nazis blamed the Jews for starting the war. After ***1941*** all Jews had to wear a yellow Star of David. Then in ***1941***, in Russia, Nazi soldiers began to shoot the Jews. Millions were killed. In other parts of Europe, Jews were sent to concentration camps, and made to work until they died.

The 'Final Solution'

In ***1942***, the Nazis invented their 'final solution' to their Jewish 'problem'. All the Jews in Europe – 11 million of them – had to be put to death, they said. They sent them to death camps, and there 6 million were gassed.

SOURCE B

1. A Jew cannot be a German citizen.
2. He cannot vote.
3. He cannot work for the government.
4. Germans and Jews cannot marry.

▲ ***Some of the Nuremberg Laws.***

SOURCE C

▲ ***These Jewish people are being made to scrub the pavement, 1938.***

Tasks

1. Using pages 68–69, list the EIGHT dates in the story, noting what happened by each date.

2. Explain to a partner how things got worse for the Jews.

3. Design a poster: 'It must NEVER happen again'.

Use words and images from these pages to make a powerful poster which gets your message across.

The Diary of Anne Frank

We know how Nazi persecution affected ordinary Jews from the *Diary* of a young Dutch girl, Anne Frank.

The Nazis conquered Holland in 1940. They made life hard for Jewish people (**Source D**). Then, in 1942, they started to send Jewish people to the concentration camps. On 8 July 1942, Anne was told that the SS had 'called up' her sister Margot. She knew what would happen.

The secret house

Mr Frank had a factory, with a secret house in it – the 'door' was hidden behind a bookcase. The family went to hide there.

And there the family stayed, with another family they knew (the van Pels). Mr Frank's friends took food to them – they were very brave, because they would be sent to prison if they were found out.

The Diary

Anne was 13 years old. She could not go out. She could not look out of the window, in case someone saw her. She could not use the toilet during the day, in case someone heard her. All the family did was listen to the news on the radio – over and over again. Anne got bored.

Anne often fell out with her mother. She fell in love with Peter, the van Pels' 15-year-old son, who was hiding with them.

And she wrote her *Diary*.

SOURCE A

My 3rd hobby is history. I can hardly wait for the day I can go and read some history books in a public library.

▲ **Diary** ***of Anne Frank, for Thursday, 6 April 1944.***

SOURCE B

▲ ***A Nazi concentration camp. Anne knew what happened there.***

SOURCE C

I want to go on living even after I die. So I am glad that I can write. When I write, I am happy and brave again. But this is the question: will I ever write anything great? I want to be a writer when I grow up.

▲ ***Diary of Anne Frank, Tuesday, 4 April 1944.***

NEW WORDS

radio, bored, library

Hopes of freedom

On 6 June 1944, the family heard that Allied troops had landed in Normandy. The Nazis were losing the war. Soon they would be safe. Anne wrote, 'Friends are coming. I am filled with hope. I may be back at school in September!'

A week later Anne had her 15th birthday. One of her presents was a pot of jam. 'Everything is going well!' she wrote.

Belsen

Soon after, Anne's *Diary* ends. On 4 August 1944, the Nazis found the secret house. Peter and the grown-ups were sent to Auschwitz death camp, where all but Mr Frank died. Anne and Margot were sent to Belsen, where they fell ill. Anne died, some time during March 1945.

A month later, British soldiers captured the camp and freed the prisoners.

SOURCE D

Our family felt the full impact of Hitler's anti-Jewish laws, and life was filled with worry. After May 1940, the good times fled. Jews must wear a yellow star. Jews must hand in their bikes. Jews are banned from trams. Jews can only go shopping between 3 and 5 o'clock. Jews must be indoors by 8 o'clock.

So we could not do this and we were not allowed to do that. But life went on in spite of it all.

Diary *of Anne Frank, for Saturday, 20 June 1942.*

SOURCE E

British troops force German people to walk round a concentration camp, 1945.

Tasks

1. Why, do you think, did the British army make Germans go to see the death camps (**Source E**)?

2. It is more than fifty years after the war. Should we try to forgive and forget about these things now?

3. Using the list of events on pages 68–69, write an imaginary diary as if *you* were a Jew.

13 END OF EMPIRE

IN THIS CHAPTER YOU WILL LEARN:

- **THREE problems facing newly independent countries;**
- **SEVEN problems facing South Africa today.**

NEW WORDS

- independence
- corrupt
- panic
- cockroaches
- refugees

SOURCE A

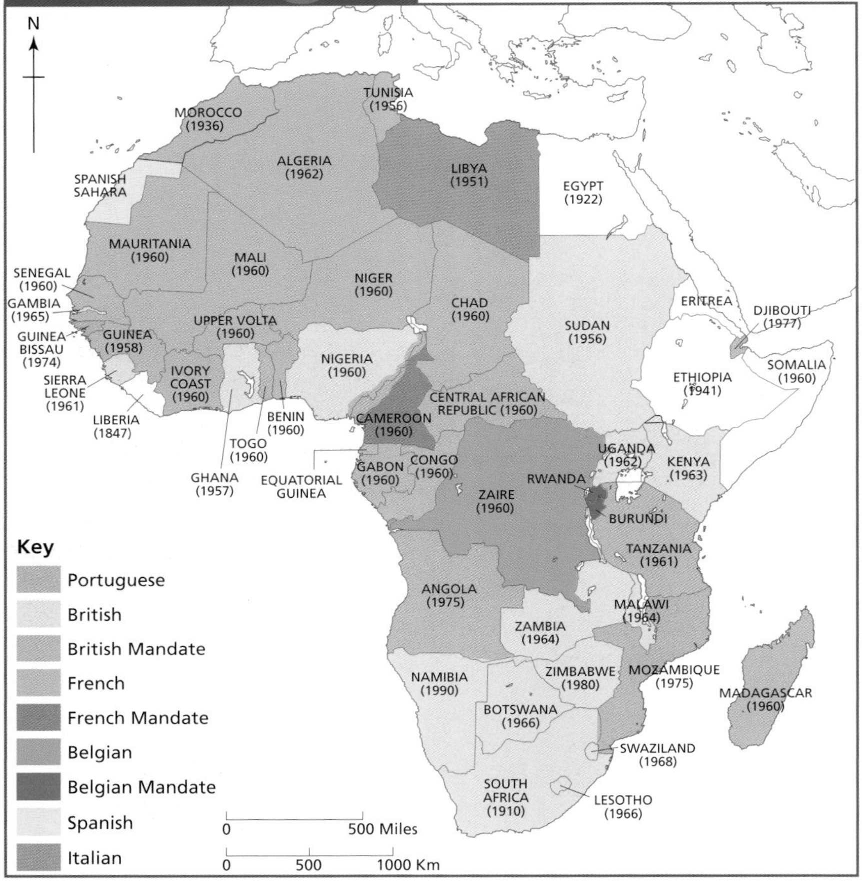

This map of Africa shows the dates that African countries gained their independence.

Q ● Think of reasons why colonies would want to be independent.

The end of Empire

Before the Second World War, Britain, France and Belgium had ruled huge empires (especially in Africa). After 1945, they gave those empires away. India and Pakistan got their independence in 1947.

Where the European rulers did not go, people often fought for their freedom. Most African countries got independence in the 1960s. In 1939, only ONE African country was fully independent; by 1980 they were ALL independent.

Problems for the new countries

Things have not gone smoothly for many of the new countries.

1. Many of them are very poor.

2. Their governments are sometimes cruel or corrupt.

3. There have been civil wars and rebellions.

An Example: Rwanda

From 1919 to 1962, Rwanda in Africa was a Belgian colony with farmers (Hutus), and cattle-owners (Tutsis). The Belgians said the two groups were different races, and gave out cards saying that people were 'Hutu' or 'Tutsi'. Rwanda got independence in 1962. A Hutu government was elected. It persecuted the Tutsis. Some Hutus said that Hutus should not marry Tutsis – that Tutsis were cheats, cockroaches and enemies.

But, as they attacked the Tutsis, the Hutus became frightened that the Tutsis would rebel. In 1994, in a wave of panic, the Hutus took clubs and knives, went house-to-house, and mass-murdered every Tutsi they could find. The rivers ran red with blood.

But, when a Tutsi army fought back, a million Hutus fled the country in panic. Thousands died of hunger or disease in refugee camps. It was one of the biggest human disasters of the century.

SOURCE C

A teenage boy fighting in Africa. Rebel armies in Africa have trained children to become mass-murderers.

There are 54 countries in Africa. Since they became independent, 11 have had civil wars, and 32 have had army take-overs. Only 2 have stayed peaceful democracies all the time.

SOURCE B

Saudi Arabia 2.7
Norway 1.1
Sweden 0.9
France 0.8
Belgium 0.4
Britain 0.3

This shows how much of their income these rich countries give to poor countries. The United Nations says that rich countries should give 0.7%. Which is the worst country of all?

Tasks

1. Copy out the 'three problems facing independent countries'. Ask your teacher to give you examples of these problems.

2. Whose fault was the disaster in Rwanda? Should we give aid to the Hutu refugees?

The end of apartheid

Q

- Put these aspirations in order of how important they are to you:

  A nice house
  A good job
  The vote
  A good car
  A good time.

Nelson Mandela before he was put in prison in 1960, and after he was set free in 1991.

Election Day

On 26 April 1994, there was an election in South Africa. Nearly 22 million people went to vote.

Some people walked 60 miles, and waited for days, to cast their vote.

Under apartheid, most swimming pools and buses could only be used by whites. A black person sitting on a 'whites only' beach could go to prison for 5 years.

SOURCE A

There was no other way to oppose *apartheid*. All the lawful ways of opposing it had been banned by the government. We could accept for ever that we were not as good as the whites – or we could fight. We chose to fight.

Nelson Mandela explains why he used violence after 1961.

Apartheid

Since 1948, South Africa had been ruled by the policy of apartheid – the white government said that whites and blacks should stay apart.

Apartheid was really just a way of keeping power and money for the whites. The black peoples of South Africa were given 'homelands' to live in, but they were the poorest parts of the country. Half the blacks in South Africa still lived in white areas – they worked for the white businessmen. Blacks had to carry a passbook which said who they were and where they should be. If black people protested, the police beat and tortured them. Sometimes – for example at Sharpeville in 1960 – they shot them dead. After this, some blacks (led by a lawyer called Nelson Mandela) turned to violence. Mandela was arrested and put in prison.

During the 1980s, the violence got worse. Many countries stopped trading with South Africa in protest at apartheid.

Freedom

The white government knew it would have to change. Mandela was set free. Apartheid was abolished.

The 1994 election was the first election in which blacks could vote. They elected Nelson Mandela.

In 1994, *Nkosi Sikelel' iAfrica* ('God bless Africa' – the song of the black protesters) became the South African national anthem.

SOURCE C

This teenage boy was killed when police shot at protesting school-children in 1976.

SOURCE B

Police use whips to attack protesters in the 1970s.

Problems facing South Africa

Population: 50 million

- 23 million people have no electricity.
- 15 million do not have a toilet.
- The black unemployment rate is 40%.
- The 6 million whites still own 75% of the country's wealth.
- Two-thirds of black people did not finish their education.
- Many black Zulu people want independence.
- Some white people have joined a Nazi-style AWB party.

NEW WORDS

Apartheid: the policy that blacks and whites should stay apart.

election, accept, violence

Tasks

1. Reading pages 74–75, do you want to change your answer to question 1?

2. Was Nelson Mandela right to start to use violence?

3. Look at the SEVEN 'problems facing South Africa' on page 75. Go through the list, discussing for each why it is a problem, what needs to be done, and what will happen if nothing is done about it.

14 WHO STARTED THE COLD WAR?

IN THIS CHAPTER YOU WILL LEARN:

- THREE causes of the Cold War;
- THREE crises of the Cold War.

The Cold War

America and Russia had fought on the same side against Hitler, but as soon as he was defeated, they fell out.

The atomic bomb stopped them going to war against each other. If they had gone to war, they would had wiped each other out.

So, instead, they had a 'Cold' War – they did everything they could to hurt each other, but they did not start fighting.

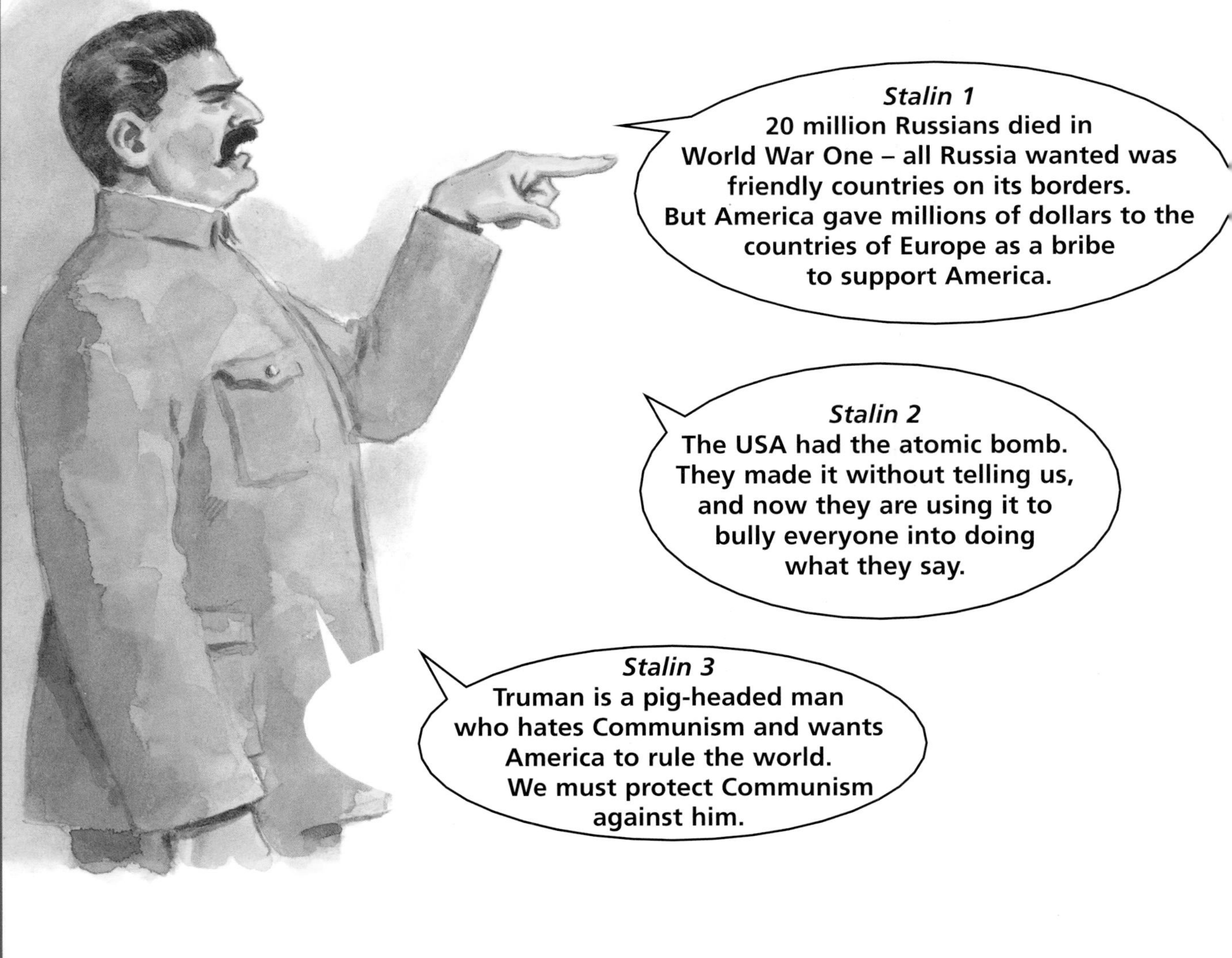
Stalin 1
20 million Russians died in World War One – all Russia wanted was friendly countries on its borders. But America gave millions of dollars to the countries of Europe as a bribe to support America.
Stalin 2
The USA had the atomic bomb. They made it without telling us, and now they are using it to bully everyone into doing what they say.
Stalin 3
Truman is a pig-headed man who hates Communism and wants America to rule the world. We must protect Communism against him.

Tasks

1. Using the speech bubbles, act out the clash between Truman and Stalin – what THREE things did they disagree about?

2. Who, do you think, was most to blame for the Cold War?

3. Using the speech bubbles, talk with a partner about how these things helped to cause the Cold War:

- Eastern Europe
- Armies and weapons
- Different beliefs.

Truman 1
After the war, Russia took over many of the countries in Eastern Europe, one after the other. It was the start of a plot to take over the world.
Truman 2
America gave money aid to the countries of Europe to stop people starving after the war. Russia put huge armies into the countries of Eastern Europe to control them.
Truman 3
Communism is evil, and Stalin is a cruel tyrant who wants to take over the world. We must make the world safe for democracy.

Three crises of the Cold War

Berlin Crisis, 1948–49

By 1948 the Russians controlled all of eastern Europe (**Source A**). The border between eastern Europe and free western Europe was called 'the Iron Curtain'. West Berlin was the only place behind the Iron Curtain which was not communist.

SOURCE **A**

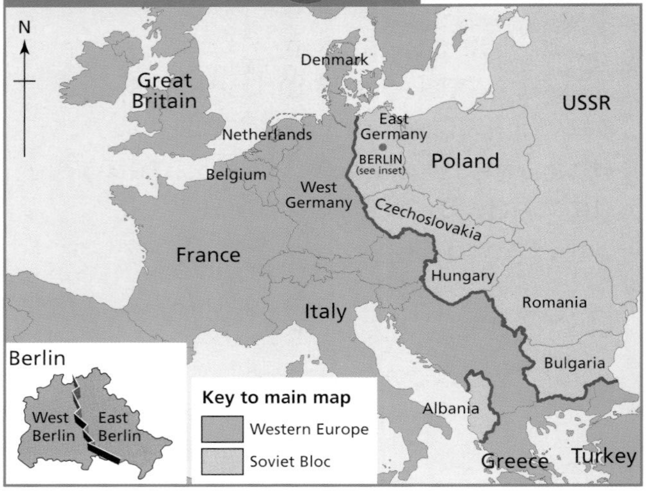

A map of Europe in 1948. In 1948, West Berlin was a little island of freedom behind the Iron Curtain. ➤

SOURCE **B**

◀ ***This Russian cartoon shows US and British and American soldiers goose-stepping like Nazis. What did the Russians think the Americans were doing in the Cold War?***

Q ● Who won the Berlin Crisis?

In 1948 Stalin closed the borders around West Berlin. West Berlin was cut off. No food could get in. Stalin hoped to take over.

For 11 months US and British bombers flew tons of supplies into West Berlin. In 1949, Stalin gave up. West Berlin survived.

NEW WORDS

nuclear missile base

The Korean War, 1950–53

Korea was split into North and South Korea. In 1950, Communist North Korea attacked democratic South Korea. By September 1950, they had captured almost all the country.

Led by the Americans, the United Nations sent an army to help the South Koreans. The Chinese joined the war on the side of the North Koreans. They drove the American army back. When the war ended in 1953, everything was back to where it all started!

Q ● Who won the Korean War?

The Cuba Crisis, 1962

Cuba was a communist country, but it was less than 150 miles from the USA! The Americans were worried about Cuba.

On 14 October 1962, a US spy plane spotted that the Russians were building a nuclear missile base on Cuba. And a Russian ship carrying nuclear missiles was on its way to Cuba.

John F. Kennedy, the American President, told Russia to stop. The Russians refused. On 22 October Kennedy told the US Navy to stop every Russian ship going to Cuba.

SOURCE C

An American poster. What did the Americans think they were doing in the Cold War?

Q

- 'We were afraid of you. You were afraid of us.' Do you agree with this Russian man's explanation of the Cold War?

SOURCE D

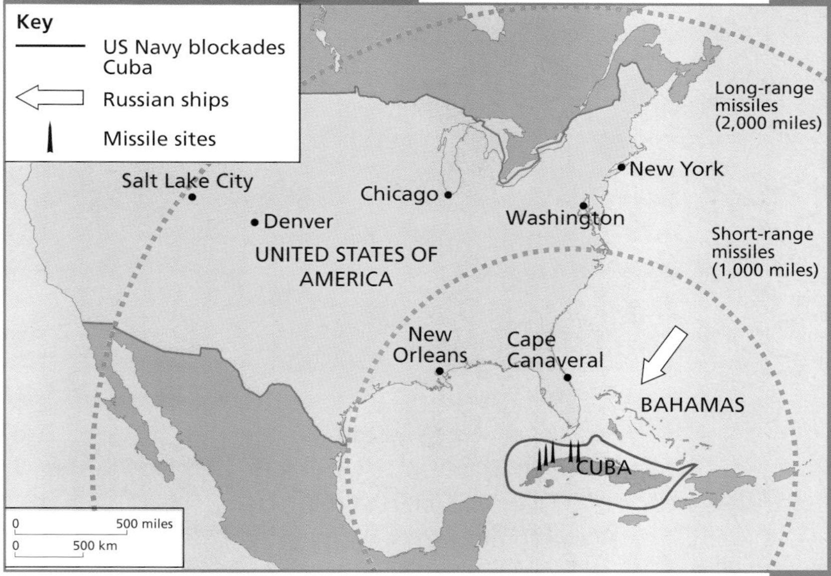

Map of the Cuba Crisis.

For six days, the Russian ships kept sailing towards Cuba. It looked as though there was going to be a Third World War. It would be an atomic war. It would wipe out humanity. Everyone was very frightened.

Then, on 28 October 1962, the Russians backed down. They destroyed the missile bases in Cuba. And the ships turned back.

In return, Kennedy promised to destroy some American missile bases in Turkey.

Some good did come from this crisis. The Americans and Russians set up a special 'hot line' telephone, so that they could talk directly if there were ever such a problem again.

Task

Using pages 78–79, write 10 questions you could ask on 'The Crises of the Cold War'. Swap them with a friend, and answer each other's questions.

15 GLOBAL COLD WAR: 1960–80

IN THIS CHAPTER YOU WILL LEARN:

- **FOUR conflicts of the Cold War;**
- **FIVE reasons the Americans lost the War in Vietnam.**

America and Russia dared not go to war. So they fought each other at second hand – they sent money, weapons and 'military advisers' to help 'their' side in conflicts all over the world.

1

In Central and South America, the US helped cruel and corrupt anti-Communist dictators who killed hundreds of their own people to stay in power.

▲ This protest in London was held by the family and friends of people who had 'disappeared' in Chile.

2

In many African countries there were wars between different tribes or groups.

Instead of trying to stop these wars, America and Russia kept them going, and gave help to the different sides.

▲ These up-to-date Russian missiles are in Ethiopia, one of the poorest countries in the world.

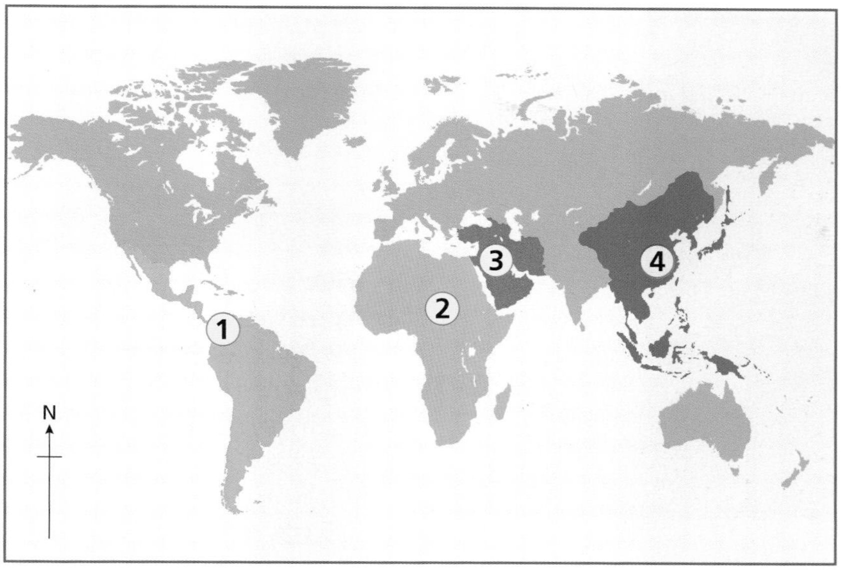

Tasks

1. List FOUR bad effects of the Cold War.

2. Design a poster with the message 'Cold War Costs Too Much!

3

In the Middle East there were wars between the Jewish state of Israel, and the Arab countries round it.

The Americans supported Israel. The Russians supported the Arabs.

This 'supergun' was being built by Iraq to fire a nuclear missile. It is possible that Israel has nuclear weapons.

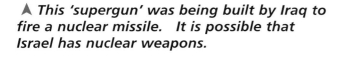

4

The Americans fought a long war in Vietnam, trying to stop South Vietnam being conquered by the Communist North Vietnamese (who were helped by Russia and China).

In Cambodia, China supported a ruler called Pol Pot who murdered millions of his own people.

This picture shows the skulls of people murdered in Cambodia.

The United Nations: success or failure?

SOURCE A

UN soldiers trying to keep the peace in Bosnia in the 1990s (see cutting 7).

NEW WORDS

WHO: World Health Organisation.
WFP: World Food Programme.
IMF: International Monetary Fund.
FAO: Food and Agriculture Organisation.
inoculate, locusts

The United Nations

The United Nations was set up in 1945. Its aims are to keep world peace, and to make people's lives better. These 'newspaper cuttings' are just a small part of what the UN has done.

1. October 1955

No End to Apartheid

The United Nations today told South Africa to end apartheid. South Africa left the UN, and apartheid goes on.

2. Jan 1963

UN forces set to leave Congo

UN troops are leaving the Congo. They have been in Africa since 1960, when the Belgians left the Congo, taking everything with them. The UN has run the country, kept hospitals open and trained doctors and teachers.

3. March 1964

UN keeps peace in Cyprus

After months of fighting, Greeks and Turks have made peace in Cyprus. UN troops will guard the ceasefire line.

4. Jan 1977

UN Saves Temples

The United Nations' organisation UNESCO has stepped in to save Greek temples in Athens, which are being destroyed by traffic.

5. 1979

Smallpox is Dead – Official

The United Nations' WHO said today that it had killed smallpox. The WHO has been inoculating people since 1948.

SOURCE B

UN food trucks drive through a war zone in Africa in 1994. Many people were saved from starving to death.

SOURCE C

The United Nations cannot force people to stop fighting.

U Thant, the head of the United Nations, speaking about the Vietnam War.

6. April 1994

UN feeds 'city' in Congo

One day after 250,000 refugees fled from Rwanda, the United Nations' WFP is sending enough food to feed them.

7. July 1995

Bosnian Withdrawal

UN forces today pulled out of Zepa in Bosnia. The UN had been trying to protect the town as part of a ceasefire agreement, but the Serbs would not stop attacking.

8. January 1997

UNICEF combats Child Prostitution

Workers for UNICEF (which looks after children) came to Thailand today to stop child prostitution. They will help the government write new laws, and will run education and aid programmes.

9. December 1997

UN saves Seoul

A loan of $21 billion from the United Nations' IMF today saved the economy of South Korea from disaster. IMF experts are now working with the government to make sure it never happens again.

10. April 1998

Africa at War – with locusts

60 million locusts have attacked crops in Madagascar. The UN FAO has sent in planes to spray them.

SOURCE D

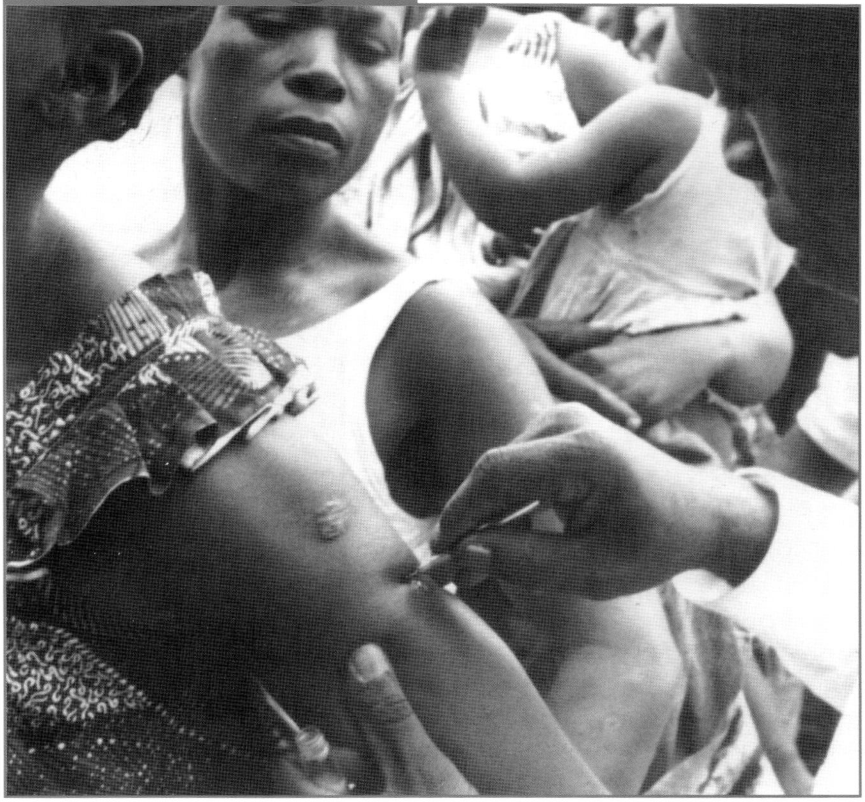

A UN doctor inoculates a woman in the Congo in 1960. The UN is working to bring health to all.

Tasks

1. Make a list of the kind of work done by UNESCO, the WHO, the WFP, UNICEF, the IMF and the FAO. How good is the UN at improving people's lives?

2. Look at cuttings 2, 3 and 7. How good is the UN at keeping the peace?

INVESTIGATION

Why did the US lose the Vietnam War?

***Your Mission:** to organise a demonstration against the Vietnam War.*

NEW WORDS

guerrilla war: a war fought by ambush.

napalm: a sticky petrol-based jelly that burns people to death.

demand

The Vietnam War

In the 1960s, the Americans tried to stop the Communist armies of North Vietnam conquering South Vietnam. They failed. In 1973, they pulled out of Vietnam.

The Americans failed because:

1. Their troops were not used to fighting in the jungle.
2. The Vietcong had good Russian and Chinese weapons.
3. The Vietcong fought a guerrilla war.
4. The Vietcong were helped by the ordinary people and hid among them.
5. Americans saw the war on TV and demanded that it end.

***1.** The South Vietnamese soldiers often tortured or shot prisoners.*

***2.** Students protesting the war. Young Americans were called up to go and fight. Many did not want to go. Those who refused were sent to prison.*

***3.** Children burned by napalm. This ordinary village had been bombed by accident. The Americans dropped 7 million tons of bombs on Vietnam.*

4. 2 million Vietnamese people were killed in the war. At the village of Mai Lai American soldiers murdered ordinary people.

5. Dead American soldiers coming home in body bags. 50,000 American soldiers were killed in Vietnam.

6. The war cost so much that the government stopped building new houses.

7. In 1968 – when the Americans thought they were winning the war – the Vietcong fought back in an all-out attack. It made the Americans realise they could never win.

Tasks

1. Imagine you are a student protesting the war. Talk with a friend about the pictures you have seen on the TV (pictures 1–7). For each, discuss how it makes the war a bad war.

2. After seeing these pictures on the TV you decide to:

a. make up an anti-war slogan to shout (it must have two short lines which rhyme).

b. design a banner to carry.

c. write a short speech on why the war is wrong. Talk about how:

- ordinary people are suffering;
- American troops are behaving;
- the South Vietnamese behave;
- the cost of the war;
- America is going to lose;
- young people do not want to go.

16 A CHANGING WORLD

IN THIS CHAPTER YOU WILL LEARN:
- **FIVE reasons Communism failed;**
- **FIVE problems in Russia after the fall of Communism.**

Problems in Russia
By the 1980s, Russia was weak. Its factories were out-of-date. People were angry that they did not have as much money or as much freedom as people in America.

Reform and Revolution
In 1985, a leader called Mikhail Gorbachev came to power. He:

1. allowed free enterprise;

2. gave the Russian people greater freedom;

3. stopped Russia's nuclear arms race with America.

Many old Communists in Russia hated Gorbachev, and in 1991 they kidnapped him and tried to take over the country. But their revolution failed. Thousands of ordinary people went onto the streets and protested. The army refused to attack them.

The protests were led by Boris Yeltsin. Soon after, Yeltsin became President of Russia.

Eastern Europe
Before 1988, in Eastern Europe, when there had been protests against Communism, the Russian army had put them down. But by 1988, the Russian army was in trouble. It did not have enough money to pay its soldiers. Russia began to pull its army out of its bases in Eastern Europe. So 1989 became known as the 'year of revolutions' – there were revolutions against Communism in ALL the countries of Eastern Europe. The new governments brought in Western-style democracy and free enterprise.

NEW WORDS

free enterprise: when businesses are privately-owned – not run by the government.

Russian workers often refused to work hard because their wages were so low. They said, 'You pretend to pay us, so we will pretend to work.'

Tasks

1. Give TWO reasons the Communist counter-revolution of 1991 failed.

2. Using the information in the Ideas File on page 87, list FIVE weaknesses of Communism in Russia.

3. Look at Gorbachev's reforms (*lines 9–12*). Which weaknesses did each reform hope to correct?

IDEAS FILE: WHY DID COMMUNISM FAIL?

1. Workers became lazy because the government gave everybody a job, no matter how hard they worked.

2. In Communist countries, factories were run by the government, which often had no idea of what was needed.

3. Russia's Communist leaders were corrupt. They had the best houses and lots of money, while ordinary people had nothing.

4. The Communist countries of Eastern Europe found it hard to get rich, because they had been ruined by the Second World War.

5. Russia spent too much money on the arms race with America. The government did not spend money on modern machinery for the factories.

China is different

For a while, it seemed that things would be the same in China. The Chinese government tried to get on better with America and Britain. It allowed some free enterprise.

In 1989, thousands of students met in Peking, asking for democracy. Would Communism fall in China, too?

The government told the army to attack the protesters. *It did* – 1000 students were killed. China stayed a Communist country.

Task

- Why did Communism fail in Russia and Eastern Europe, but survive in China – what was the big difference?

The Berlin Wall

17 August 1962

On Monday morning, 17 August 1962, a 17-year-old East German bricklayer called Peter Fechter got out of bed, got dressed, and left the house. But he did not go to work. He went into the centre of Berlin.

In 1961, the East German government had built a concrete wall across the centre of Berlin. Many people did not like living in Communist East Germany – every year, $^1/_4$ million East Germans had escaped by going into West Berlin. The Wall was built to stop them.

Peter Fechter wanted to live in West Germany. He and his friend Helmut Kulbeik went to a place where the guards could not see them, and climbed to the top of the Wall. Then they dropped down into the no-man's land between the Wall and West Berlin.

But two East German guards – Rolf Friedrich and Erich Schreiber – opened fire. They could not really see the men, but they fired 24 shots. Kulbeik escaped, but Fechter was hit.

Peter Fechter lay there for 50 minutes. 'Help me!' he kept shouting. West Berliners threw him bandages, but they were afraid they would be shot by the East Germans if they went to help. The East German guards did nothing – they were afraid they would be shot by the West Germans.

So Peter Fechter bled to death.

SOURCE A

A West Berlin family waves across the wall to relatives trapped in East Berlin.

NEW WORDS

bricklayer, escaped, bandages

SOURCE B

17 August 1962. East German guards take away Peter Fechter's body. West Berliners chanted 'Murderers!' In all, 86 people died trying to escape across the Berlin Wall.

9 November 1989

On the night of 9 November 1989, big crowds met on both sides of the Berlin Wall. Then people went and started to break down the wall with picks and hammers.

Everyone knew that the East German government was about to fall. The Wall guards looked on. They did not know what to do. So they did nothing. And the Wall came down.

Within a year, Germany was united, and East Germany was free.

SOURCE C

Berlin, November 1989: the Wall comes down.

SOURCE D

I am sorry about what happened.

Rolf Friedrich's letter to the family of Peter Fechter.

The East German police spies were the best – or worst – in the world. They had files on almost everyone – including little glass jars of people's smells. They even had files on Friedrich and Schreiber!

After the war, West German police found a copy of a letter in which Schreiber said he shot Fechter – so 35 years later, on 3 March 1997, he was put on trial for Fechter's murder.

Tasks

1. Write three imaginary letters:

a. from Peter Fechter to his family, explaining what he was about to do and why;

b. from Rolf Freidrich to Fechter's family, explaining what happened and why, from *his* point of view.

c. from a West Berlin housewife (who had seen the events), to a relative in East Germany, explaining what happened and why, from her point of view.

2. Should Rolf Freidrich be tried for murder?

Is life better after Communism?

***Your Mission:* to prepare a Communist election manifesto.**

NEW WORDS

replace, power station, pollution

The good news . . . and the bad

In many ways, the fall of Communism was good news for Russia and the countries of Eastern Europe. Now they had freedom, democracy and free enterprise.

But, in some ways, things have got worse since the old Communist governments fell.

Here is the news . . .

Today, war has broken out in the former Russian state of Chechnya.

New governments have replaced the Communist government, but they cannot keep control of the country.

It was found yesterday that a Russian power station is causing hu
pollution problems.

Russia's out-of-date factories are unsafe and unhealthy. To bring them up-to-date will cost millions of pounds

A special report today on Russia's street beggars.

The Communist governments gave work for everyone. Under free enterprise, many workers have lost their jobs.

More trouble in Russia today as another gangland killing rocks Russia.

Crime in Russia has run out of control. Gangsters do as they like, now the Communist police force has been closed down.

A sad meeting today, as many Russians get AIDS.

Russia has opened up to the West. Russia now has CocaCola and MacDonalds . . . and AIDS and drugs.

Tasks

1. List the FIVE problems of Russia after the fall of Communism.

2. Imagine you are a Communist who wants to go back to the old system. Write a manifesto, complaining about what is wrong, and saying what you would do to change things back.

INVESTIGATION

Have the challengers won?

Your Mission: to see if things changed in the 20th century.

Challengers

In 1900 certain groups of people held all the power; others wanted it. Three such groups were:

- black people
- women
- anti-colonialists.

Q Compare the modern pictures, with the pictures from the start of the century.

- How much has the world changed for these people?
- What is still the same?
- Have the challengers won?

▲ **Picture 1** *Black soldiers fighting in World War One* *(see page 48).*

SOURCE A

▲ ***General Colin Powell was the top general in the US Army in the Gulf War. Many people said he should stand for President, but his family would not let him – they were afraid that he would be killed.***

◄ **Picture 2** *Nancy Astor* *(see page 50).*

SOURCE B

Women Labour MPs with Tony Blair in 1997. The Labour Party wanted more women to stand for Parliament. In 1997, out of a total of 659 MPs, 120 were women. ►

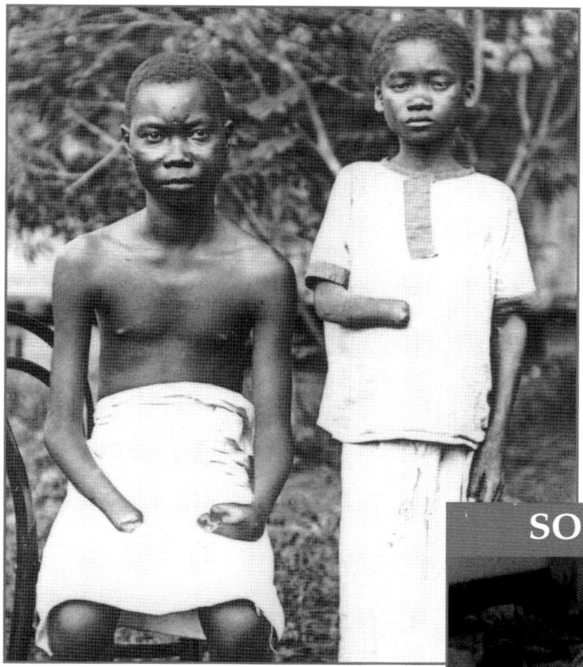

▲ **Picture 3** *African workers punished in the Congo* *(see page 3).*

In the 20th century, world population grew fourfold. We spend 20 times as much money. In 1900, about 1 billion people were starving; the number was the same in 1998.

SOURCE **C**

People killed in Rwanda. ▼

Tasks

Make a newspaper, ***20th Century News***.

Look back through this book and choose stories to run under the following headlines:

- 'The Greatest Ruler'
- 'Biggest War Story'
- 'Biggest Disaster'
- 'Politics Page'
- 'Woman's Page'
- 'Human Interest'.
- 'The Worst Ruler'
- 'Worst Atrocity'
- 'Greatest Change'
- 'Health Page'
- 'A Place to Visit'

Index

Tasks

1 Go through the list of 'People'. Can you remember what they were famous for? Look them up and see if you were right.

2 Go through the index entries 'Events'. Can you remember what happened? Look them up and see if you were right.

3 Go through the index entry 'Cold War'. For each crisis, find out when it happened, and what happened.

4 Use the index to find out:
- when did South Africa introduce the policy of *apartheid*?
- Who did the *Ku Klux Klan* attack?
- What did the *Treaty of Versailles* say?

5 Use the index to find out about either:

The First World War, Jews, the Second World War OR Women.

Use what you have found to do a project, with writing and drawings.